Simple
Scrapbooks

the scrapbooker's
Almanac

by Elizabeth Dillow

This book is dedicated to:

Matt, for his never-ending support and patience through such a monumental project

Maddie and **Gracie**, for the size of their spirits and the depth of their inspiration

Bridget, who arrived too late to appear in these pages much, but who was with me from the very beginning all the same

GET READY TO BE INSPIRED

W hen was the last time you became so engrossed in something that you lost track of time? I first saw pages and projects for this book in the *Simple Scrapbooks* photo studio, where they were being propped and photographed. As I flipped through albums and read journaling on layouts, I found myself completely entranced—so much so that I had to be summoned to a meeting, late!

I know you'll feel the same. The talented Elizabeth Dillow has created a compendium of amazing ideas—all based on events from the calendar—that will empower you in the quest for more meaningful scrapbooks. People like Elizabeth don't come along every day. She has a gift for conceptualizing poignant projects, for thoughtfully choosing her words, and for designing with intentional simplicity. I am often drawn to her work in *Simple Scrapbooks* magazine and have borrowed elements from her pages many times.

In fact, the layout below is a "scraplift" of Elizabeth's layout on page 118—the first of several ideas from this book that will make their way into my own scrapbooks. But beyond the beautiful page designs, this book has motivated me to look at my calendar with new eyes, discovering meaningful inspiration in the holidays and historical events that come around year after year. In my opinion, this is the freshest resource of original ideas to hit the scrapbooking world in a long, long time!

Stacy

STACY JULIAN
Founding Editor,
Simple Scrapbooks magazine

P.S. *National Author's Day is November 1, so why not make a layout about all your favorite authors? I bet Elizabeth Dillow will make your list!*

al·ma·nac |ál·mə·nak| noun

· an annual calendar containing important dates and statistical information, such as astronomical data or tide tables*

· a handbook, typically published annually, containing information of general interest or on a sport or pastime

scrapbooker's almanac |skráp·ük·ərz * ál·mə·nak| proper noun

· a month-by-month guide that helps scrapbookers draw inspiration from events on the calendar—from Arbor Day to Ansel Adams's Birthday to National Cancer Survivors' Day

I love calendars. I am heartened by all the tidy little squares marching endlessly on into the future, each holding infinite possibilities within the boundaries of 24 hours. When I was a high school history teacher (just a handful of years ago), my life revolved around the calendar. Everything we studied originated from one of those little squares—marking the anniversary of a significant event, or the birth of an important person, or the genesis of a revolutionary idea. While these historical events may seem distant sometimes, they're really not when you realize that every year you get to meet up with them again like old friends.

In *The Scrapbooker's Almanac*, my talented contributors and I discovered meaningful new ways to get inspired by the calendar. In total, we created 103 scrapbook pages and projects, all inspired by events that someone, somewhere remembers and honors every year. But for every national observance, birthday, or anniversary recognized in the pages that follow, there are hundreds more left out. Luckily, there will always be another year, when we can sit down with a blank calendar and see what inspires us then. I hope you'll find enough inspiration in this book to keep you scrapbooking through this calendar year and many more to come. But above all, I hope you'll have fun along the way!

Elizabeth

*You'll find no astronomical data or tide tables in this book, but there will be plenty of talk about pretty paper. Hopefully this does not influence your decision to read further.

How to use this book

I love lists as much as I love calendars, so here's a list of random thoughts to help you get the most out of this book:

circa 34

1. By all means, feel free to replicate your favorite pages and projects from this book! A wise woman once said you don't apologize to dinner guests for following a recipe to create a meal. I don't know about you, but I have better things to do with my time than reinvent the wheel every time I sit down to scrapbook!

2. Not interested in baseball? Can't stand '80s music? Prefer pie over cookies? No problem! Use the projects as idea generators for your own passions.

3. Stick to your own unique style. The *Simple Scrapbooks* philosophy isn't just about using minimal embellishments or finishing each page in under 30 minutes. Maybe you prefer to use 23 embellishments or 11 techniques per page—great! The *Simple* philosophy is about scrapbooking what matters to you, without guilt. So if you see a page that looks too complicated or not complicated enough, just use the idea as a foundation and build the rest any way you see fit!

4. Be inspired literally, be inspired figuratively. Either way is fine. Let your mind wander through all the possibilities of how your project could turn out and you'll no doubt create something authentic, something you can be proud of.

5. If you're anything like me, you have plenty of things vying for your precious free time. The items written on your planning calendar are the things that actually get done, so why not pencil in a few projects you want to try so you can't fill up your schedule with something else. And if you still run out of time? Remember that next year's calendars will be available well before the end of the year!

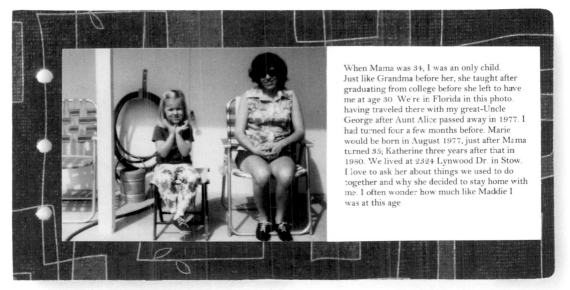

When Mama was 34, I was an only child. Just like Grandma before her, she taught after graduating from college before she left to have me at age 30. We're in Florida in this photo, having traveled there with my great-Uncle George after Aunt Alice passed away in 1977. I had turned four a few months before. Marie would be born in August 1977, just after Mama turned 35; Katherine three years after that in 1980. We lived at 2324 Lynwood Dr. in Stow. I love to ask her about things we used to do together and why she decided to stay home with me. I often wonder how much like Maddie I was at this age.

National Women's History Month inspired me to scrapbook about the women who came before me on my family tree (see page 40). How will it inspire you?

Contributors

LAURA KURZ
Baltimore, Maryland

Laura's favorite month is May and her favorite holiday, Christmas—she loves shopping for the perfect gifts (and stationery!) and spending the holiday with family and friends. She is married to Ken and mom to Charmer, a 7-year-old golden retriever. By day she is the director of communications for an independent school in Baltimore. She knew she was destined to be a scrapbooker when she spent the summer before her junior year in college studying and working in London. After purchasing an album at Paperchase, she spent the entire seven-hour plane ride home gluing postcards, photos, and memorabilia into the album—that was just the beginning!

MI'CHELLE LARSEN
Bountiful, Utah

Mi'Chelle's favorite month is September, and her favorite holiday is Valentine's Day—because deep down she's really a mushy, twitterpated 14-year-old who loves pink. She is married to Gabe and mama to Gabriella and Owen. By day Mi'Chelle is a nose-wiping, sandwich-making, blog-surfing, crafty mama. She knew she was destined to be a scrapbooker because of her lifelong love of paper, and also because of her inspiring 7th grade English teacher, Mrs. Finlinson, who had the most fabulous handwriting ever and handmade all of her classroom decorations out of cardstock. Mrs. Finlinson also liked Mi'Chelle's "scrapbookish" autobiography, thereby sealing the deal.

ANNA ASPNES
Elmendorf AFB, Alaska

Anna's favorite month changes depending on where her family is stationed (Japan, Maryland, or anywhere between!) and her favorite holiday is Christmas—for the pure magic. She is married to Eric and mum to Ella and Luke (affectionately nicknamed Luke "The Nuke"). By day she is a master multitasker who creates digital designs for a variety of major scrapbooking sites, chases two non-stop kiddos, supports her Air Force husband in both his school and career, and tries to keep her living quarters in some semblance of order. She knew she was destined to be a scrapbooker when working in Photoshop became as habitual as brushing her teeth.

MARGARET SCARBROUGH
Butte Valley, California

Margaret's favorite month is December and her favorite holiday is Christmas—because of the presents! She loves wrapping them and handing them out to all her family and friends. Margaret is married to Jack and mom to Matthew and Wesley (better known as Hoonie). By day she is a mildly successful domestic engineer. She knew she was destined to be a scrapbooker when she found a hobby that incorporated her love of paper, stickers and cute little thingamabobs.

MARY MacASKILL
Calgary, Alberta

Mary's favorite month is June and her favorite holiday is Christmas—because she loves snowflakes, frosted sugar cookies, midnight Mass, traditions, wrapping gifts, and sharing time with her family. She is married to Derrick and mom to Sadie. By day she is an environmental engineer. She knew she was destined to be a scrapbooker when she started collecting photos, magazine clippings, and poems to paste in a notebook.

Contents

For ideas, tips, and inspiration from Elizabeth Dillow all year long, visit **simplescrapbooksmag.com/almanac**.

1

2

3

4

5

6

7

8

9

10

11

12

13

14

15

16

17

18

19

20

21

22

23

24

25

26

27

28

29

30

31

This month...

forget the resolutions—focus on creativity

combat clutter with something cute

design with flowers

tell an immigrant's story

record your family's first day of the year

time-travel with music

put mountains of trivia to good use

write an old-fashioned letter to a dear friend

write by hand

THIS MONTH-LONG CREATIVITY OBSERVATION was initiated by entrepreneur Randall Munson, an author and speaker who advocates creativity as the key to success in business. His challenge to reflect upon ingenuity in the marketplace can easily be applied to all creative endeavors—and what better time to refocus on creativity than the beginning of a new year? So instead of making a list of "creative resolutions," create a visual reminder of what makes you feel most creative and display it all year long.

7 x 5 flip album

TIP: *In addition to scrapbooking, I love to construct, bind, or cover my own handmade books—it's a hobby I've enjoyed for years that complements scrapbooking well. Don't have an interest in tinkering with book bindings and Davey board? No problem! Try incorporating a technique or two from another hobby you enjoy into your scrapbook projects from time to time. Now that's a great exercise in creativity!*

helping her create helps me to create, too

m

* play piano • play often • exercise that part of the brain and watch for creative energy to come soon after

play*

wandering back and forth

PAPER SOURCE

SAN FRANCISCO
MARINA

Lori Koenig
MANAGER

2061 chestnut st.
san francisco, ca 94123

ph 415.614.1585
fx 415.614.1583

sf_manager@paper-source.com

Through the aisles as possible — throw the "law" only for current • visit card & paper stores whenever possible—spend as much time prelude, "rule out the window

ONCE UPON A TIME

read*

bobsyouruncle.com ©2004

January 1-31

National Get Organized Month

THE NATIONAL ASSOCIATION OF Professional Organizers sponsors a month-long observation each year in January to encourage people to confront their disorganized ways and make positive changes in their lives and homes.

The idea for this getting-organized project came to Mi'Chelle as she was wandering the grocery store aisles without a list—unable to remember what she needed. Mi'Chelle dreamed up a handy organizer that would be small enough to fit in her purse and cute enough to be kept by the phone. She created four chipboard dividers (titled "calendar," "menu," "to-do," and "shopping") to fit inside a 4½ x 8½ binder, which she decorated with a floral rub-on, patterned paper, and ribbon. She inserted cardstock filler pages behind each divider, giving her a place to record and store her weekly menus, shopping lists, scheduled events, and tasks. She embellished a small month-at-a-glance calendar (the size of a checkbook) as a companion piece to her binder.

TIP: *Try this technique next time you cover chipboard with patterned paper: use artist gel medium to adhere the paper, leaving ¼-inch of paper hanging over the edges. When the gel dries, use a pedicure file and sand away from the book at a 45° angle so the paper will "cut" away to the perfect size.*

4½ x 8½ binder and embellished calendar
by Mi'Chelle Larsen

First week of January

Tournament of Roses®

and Rose Parade®

that flower crown

8½ x 11 spread

DID YOU KNOW THAT EACH FLOAT CREATED FOR
the Rose Parade® (which has been held in Pasadena, California,
every January since 1890) must be designed entirely from
natural materials—primarily flowers, but also seeds bark, and
leaves? True story. While using bark on a scrapbook page is
probably not advisable, here's a simple scrapbooking challenge
inspired by the rules of the Rose Parade® that you *can* do: make
a page using only flowers as embellishments. I'm willing to bet
you have a few on hand!

BETWEEN THE PEAK IMMIGRATION YEARS OF 1892 and 1924 in the United States, hundreds of thousands of immigrants passed through Ellis Island. In fact, it's estimated that more than half of all Americans today have an ancestor who entered the U.S. through the famous site in the shadow of the Statue of Liberty. Whether or not you can trace your own ancestors through Ellis Island, January is a great month to tell the story of immigration in your own family. Create a mini-album of several relatives as Laura did, or design a page about a specific relative. It won't get any easier to collect historical details, photographs, and old family stories with each passing year—now is the time!

It all starts here...with family. My family. The Devines, the Kirks, the Hartzels. The ones who came from Ireland... The ones who tried to move cross country only to return home. The funny pictures, the serious poses. The little boy you can tell was trouble. They are a part of who I am. Let me introduce you...

TIP: *Don't be afraid of orange! Sure, it's a Halloween color, but used in the right combination, it can be so much more. Laura paired cream cardstock with orange to create an elegant and understated backdrop for her black-and-white family photographs.*

My great, great, great grandparents Patrick and Mary Ann Devine. Patrick was born in 1826 in a place called Kirkneedy, Conwal. Mary Ann was born in 1830 in the same place. They came to Philadelphia and eventually settled in Wilmington and had seven children — Hugh, Maggie, Susan, Edward, Sarah, Mame, and Lizzie.

The baby in this photo is my grandfather, Charles. It was probably taken in 1911. Katherine (Kitty) is on the far left, next to James (Jim), Ruth, and Emily on the far right. My grandmother Louise is holding Pop Pop.

My mom, JoAnn Devine, was born July 9, 1946 in Wilmington, Delaware. She is the oldest of five children — Lynn, David, Debbie, and John. She grew up in Wilmington, living in several different houses and graduated from P.S. DuPont High School. She received a degree in elementary education from The University of Delaware. After graduation, she moved to Millis, Massachusetts (a suburb of Boston) to do something different. A few years later, she moved back to the Wilmington area to teach at Avon Grove. She taught different grades, including fourth, fifth, and sixth. She met my dad in 1970 and they were married in 1971. Mutual friends introduced them. She then moved to Pittsburgh and taught there until my brother Brendan was born in 1976. She was a stay-at-home mom to us. Today, she enjoys reading, traveling, the beach, and, of course, the internet. She is a great friend and mom.

6½ x 3 mini-album
by Laura Kurz

17

January 1

New Year's Day

EVEN IF YOU DON'T HAVE SPECIFIC customs in your family, New Year's Day is an ideal occasion to create an annual tradition that sets the tone for the rest of your year.

Every year, on New Year's Day, you get dressed up in your special hanbok to perform "sebe" for ah-pah and I. This is actually an age-old Korean tradition in which the younger generation ceremoniously provides the first greeting of the new year to their elders. As you bow, you say, "Sae hae bok manhi badeu seyo," which more or less translates into "Blessings in the new year." You are also wishing them a long life. It's not a bad way to start the year for either side, actually. Especially as the bowing is often accompanied by the grown-ups throwing money (and advice)

Now that Margaret has children of her own, she is excited to share a Korean tradition called "sebe," held each January 1. This ceremonial exchange of money and advice is an age-old tradition in Korea, and it helps establish both cultural understanding and good, plain fun in the Scarbrough household. While the annual exchange only takes a few minutes, the anticipation (especially for her 7-year-old son) is what happy memories are made of.

new YeaRS Day...

to the young. Sadly, I think you've gotten quite used to making money on New Year's Day and you look forward to it every year. I guess I can't blame you, though. I know that I used to enjoy this tradition a whole lot more when I was on the receiving end of the money too! :)

TIP: Don't forget to take detail shots, like a close-up of your child's hands. Or, for a unique perspective, try focusing the camera on a small object in your child's hand, as Margaret did here. Including photos of the same event from a variety of angles is a great way to create context— every photo tells a story in its own way!

8½ x 11 page
by Margaret Scarbrough

DATE
January 4, 1936

EVENT
Billboard Chart Debut

THE BILLBOARD CHART HAS KEPT TRACK OF the music industry's most popular artists, albums, and songs for more than 70 years. If you're anything like me, this historical record of popular music serves as a time machine for different eras of your life. (And if you're a lot like me, you're embarrassed to admit you can still sing the lyrics to just about every '80s song you've ever heard.)

clearly, it was not her best year

12 x 12 page

TRY THIS: *Creating a playlist from a specific year in your life is so much fun that you'll want to make more than one. Try making a series of pages when the mood strikes; 1985 today, 2005 tomorrow, and 1992 next week. You'll be amazed at what memories come flooding back when you scan through lists of popular music!*

I love to build layouts with multiple layers of meaning. On this page, I used photographs, a traditional journaling block, a list of random memories jotted down around the page's border, and music. (Inside the CD pocket is a mix of 16 songs that connect me to strong memories from my 7th grade year.) This single page holds enough storytelling material to keep my daughters entertained for days.

DATE

January 4

EVENT

Trivia Day

7½ x 5½ tin

by Margaret Scarbrough

THE COOL THING ABOUT trivia is that nearly every topic under the sun is overflowing with little-known facts and figures just waiting to be discovered! What better occasion to capture the wealth of knowledge you or a family member possesses about a hobby, field of study, or sport than Trivia Day?

This little tin is dedicated to my six-year old son, Matthew, who at this stage in his life, dreams of becoming a real live dinosaur someday. Well, either that or a real live paleontologist (which is, of course, the next best thing to actually being a dinosaur). Matthew is, quite literally, a walking and talking encyclopedia of random prehistoric trivia...particularly as it pertains to dinosaurs. And he is also the generator of countless (make that countless, countless, countless) dinosaur drawings...complete with his own little notes and everything. I love it!

Yup, this little encyclopedia is most definitely for you Matthew. Hope you enjoy it. And thanks for contributing your wonderful artwork to it. Long live the dinosaurs (at least in this home)!

name: allosaurus
size: 40 feet / 12 meters
period: jurassic / cretaceous
location: north america
diet: carnivore (meat)
description:
Allosaurus was the largest meat-eater of the early Cretaceous period. It walked on two powerful legs and had three curved and pointed claws on each of its hands. When attacking an animal larger than itself, Allosaurus may have hunted in packs.

Collecting and categorizing interesting bits of trivia is a fun way to preserve what's important to you. Margaret's son Matthew loves dinosaurs, so she partnered with him to create an encyclopedia of knowledge that will serve as a treasured reminder of a childhood obsession.

TRY THIS: *Scrapbooking doesn't need to be a solitary sport. Encourage your children to contribute to a project like Margaret did; not only will the experience be a fun change of pace, but your little partner will also love the time, attention, and creativity!*

DATE

Second week of January

EVENT

Universal Letter

Writing Week

THIS LITTLE-KNOWN OBSERVANCE, sponsored by the International Society of Friendship and Good Will, is an effort to foster worldwide peace and understanding through friendly communication.

My friend Abby and I have been corresponding on Wednesdays for more than seven years, and in that time, we've created a treasure trove of hilarious correspondence that deserves a special place of honor. So I decorated a lunch box tin with pretty papers and embellishments to stash Abby's letters, postcards, and emails inside.

It doesn't take much to start a letter-writing tradition of your own: buy a pack of postcards or cut cardstock scraps to fit in an envelope, earmark a book of stamps just for this purpose.

and sit down for 3 minutes to write a one-line greeting. (Some of the funniest mail I've received from Abby is only one line!) Or, you could simply create a list of 12 family members or friends and make a goal to brighten 12 different mailboxes this year with something other than a bill.

TIP: Not all of my correspondence with Abby is through the U.S. mail, but it's just as easy to preserve. You can easily archive and save email to a folder on your hard drive and then burn it to a CD. Slip the CD in your box and you're done!

YOU DON'T HAVE TO HAVE JOHN Hancock-esque penmanship to include your writing on a scrapbook layout. Celebrate this founding father's birthday by making your handwriting (or someone else's) a component of your next project.

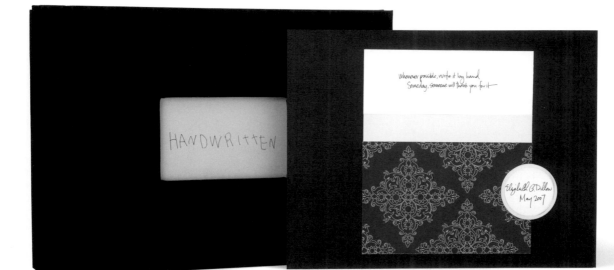

11 x 8½ album

You've heard it a thousand times before: using your own handwriting can make a page or project special, more personal. I'm not going to tell you to use your own handwriting all the time and forever abandon your treasured collection of fonts and rub-ons. (What fun would that be?) But I am going to tell you that handwriting matters, and here's why: handwriting tells a part of the story that can't be told any other way.

TIP: *My 5-year-old daughter Maddie wrote the "Handwritten" title for this album's cover. Try including your child's current penmanship on a page. In a few years, the scraggly words will be a treasure.*

charles watson

Hotel Ashtabula
ARTHUR W. GROSS, Managing Director
Ashtabula, Ohio

-/-
I have a girl named Stewart
Who's the finest in the land
And some day I hope to catch her
With that good old Wedding Band.

-2-
She's pretty, sweet & clever
In fact she can't be beat
In all my worldly travels,
Ive never seen a girl so sweet.

-3-
Although Ive known her, not for long
Its certainly my endeavor
To try & keep her Company
And have it end up never.

I never met my grandfather
Charles Watson but he left clues
about what he was like in his
scrapbook of clippings and photos
and notes and funny little captions.
He must have been a clever romantic
to have written this poem
for my Grandma before she
chose him as her own.

marie taylor

! said my Pajamas
(and put on my Pray'rs)
by Eddie Pola & George Wyle

My baby kissed me goodnight,
and I am glad to relate,
That by the time I got home
I was feeling great!

I climbed up the door, and opened the stairs;
I said my pajamas, and put on my pray'rs
I turned off the bed, and crawled into the lght;
And all because you kissed me goodnight.

By & I sang this at our
Senior Choir Concert
& our wedding ♡

If only you could
have heard Marie and B.J.
sing this song (words and music
by Eddie Pola and George Wyle,
copyright 1950) at their wedding:
she in her gown, he in his tux...
it was like something from an old
black and white movie.

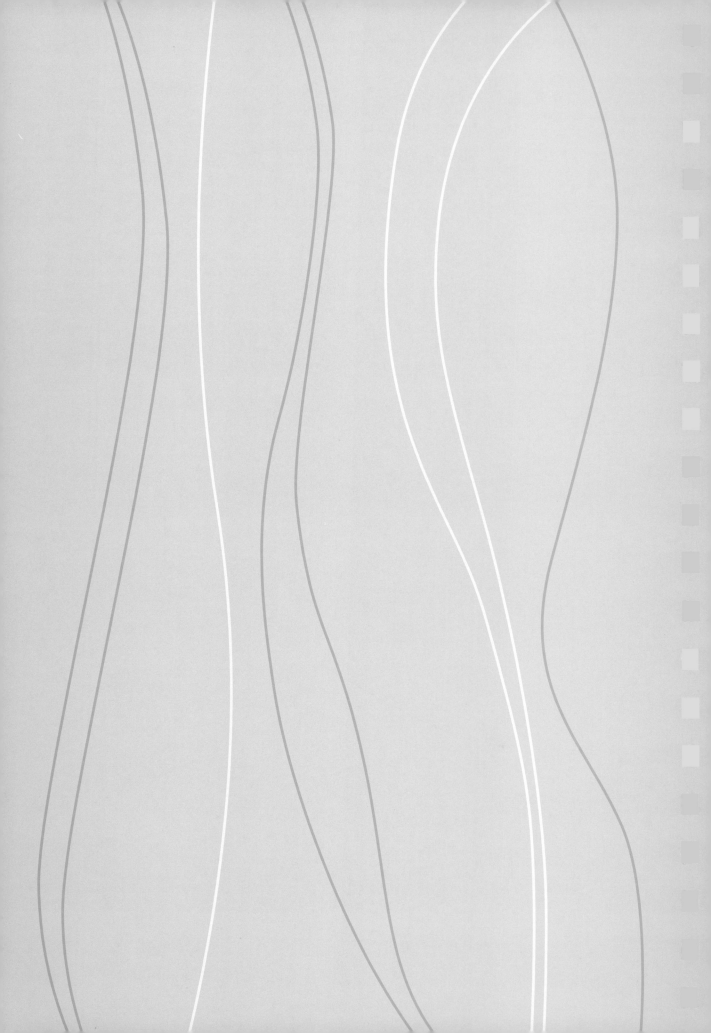

February

This month...

discover your family in the kitchen

take care of your heart

acknowledge the value of sports

revisit and relive your favorite days

listen to a master and let go of photo guilt

tell a difficult story

teach the meanings behind the celebrations

be inspired by the Man in Black

1
2
3
4
5
6
7
8
9
10
11
12
13
14
15
16
17
18
19
20
21
22
23
24
25
26
27
28
29

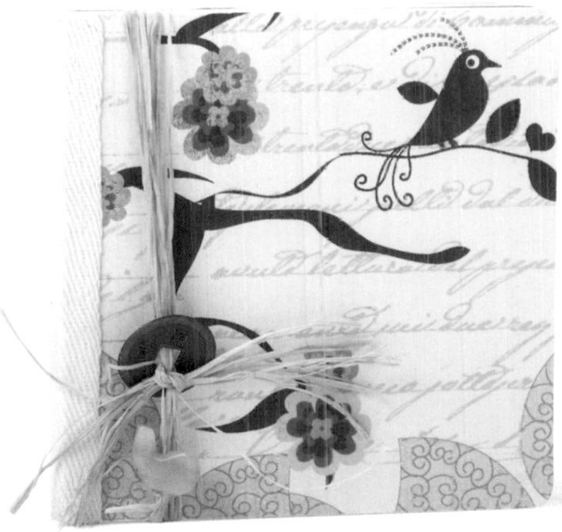

HERE'S A SIMPLE TRUTH: FAMILY HERITAGE IS intertwined with food. The favorite foods we create, the meals we share, and the memories tied to them move from generation to generation. So documenting this important aspect of family identity is a worthy task for any scrapbooker—and Bake for Family Fun Month, sponsored by the Home Baking Association, is a great reason to strengthen these natural ties.

"Devine" Cooking With Laura

Chocolate Chip Kiss Cookies

1 bag Hershey Kisses

2 sticks butter, softened

⅓ cup sugar

⅓ cup packed light brown sugar

1 teaspoon vanilla extract

2 cups flour

1 cup mini chocolate chips

- Heat oven to 375 degrees.
- Unwrap kisses.
- In large bowl, beat butter until light. Add sugar, brown sugar, and vanilla—mix again. Add flour, blend until smooth.
- Stir in mini chips. Mold a small amount of dough around each kiss, covering completely.
- Shape in balls and put on a cookie sheet.
- Bake 10–12 minutes until golden. Cool slightly before moving from cookie sheet to wire rack.
- Cool completely.

Laura chose this small album with pockets, pages, and plastic sleeves to document her family's baking traditions. By including personal anecdotes about baking with her family and stories about the recipes themselves, she created a project that is all at once a cookbook, a collection of family history, and a work of art.

I hate that I don't remember much about my mom's mom. I have the memories my mom has told me about. And I have some very hazy memories of her right before she passed away. But I'll always have her recipes. Her nut bread recipe is safely tucked away in my recipe file...In her own handwriting. Just a little piece of her.

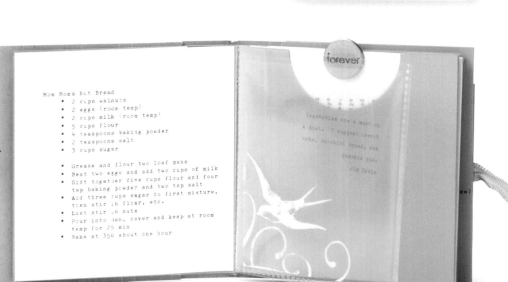

4 x 4 mini-album
by Laura Kurz

I am the lucky and grateful recipient of
many wonderful gifts from my
mother and grandmother:
   a love of books
   a love of learning
   a love of music
   a love of baseball
   a love of collecting
I am also the recipient of their
high cholesterol, but I have some
very important reasons to remember
to work hard and try to do something
about that (now don't forget)

12 x 12 page

PUT A DIFFERENT SPIN ON YOUR RED AND PINK SUPPLIES
this February by focusing on your physical heart. Cardiovascular disease is
the No. 1 cause of death in the United States each year, so there's a good
chance you or a loved one might be at risk. I know in my heart of hearts
that I need to exercise more and eat more sensibly to lower my own risk,
but it's easy to make excuses. So I display this layout to remind me of
three very important reasons to take better care of myself.

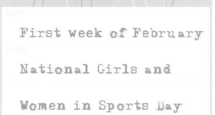

First week of February

National Girls and

Women in Sports Day

I AM A CHILD OF TITLE IX. IN 1972, JUST months before I was born, the U.S. Congress enacted legislation that prohibits discrimination in education programs and activities—especially athletics. I don't remember a time when girls didn't play sports, because in my lifetime, girls have always played sports. And played sports well.

Season 2 · Parker Hanafin 1983

Research indicates that girls who participate in sports by the age of 10 develop self-confidence, leadership skills, initiative, love of physical activity, increased health benefits throughout life, and higher levels of academic success.

10 ten

I kept playing softball season after season—from 1982–1991—because I loved batting practice, the dirt and chalk of the field, chatter, running the the first base like a locomotive, stretching to make a play at first, and my Carl Yastrzemski glove.

Anything else was just icing on the cake...

12 x 12 page

The Women's Sports Foundation seeks to celebrate female participation in athletics and underscore its importance in the development of strong, self-assured young women. I am especially fond of this photo of my 10-year-old self, full of concentration and purpose. I want my daughters to get acquainted with this girl as they flip through my scrapbooks. Do you know a girl like this?

DATE

February 2

EVENT

Groundhog Day

REMEMBER THE MOVIE *GROUNDHOG DAY*?
Bill Murray plays a weather forecaster who's stuck in a time warp in Punxsutawney, Pennsylvania, during a snowstorm on Groundhog Day. He wakes up each morning only to realize that he's reliving the same day over and over. My friend Jill was inspired by the film to make a list of five days she would willingly relive. I knew I had to come up with my own list and scrapbook it.

Red Mountain & the Symphony

5 x 5 handmade album

Matt, Jill and I set off for a full day road trip through the scenic byways of Montana, heading south on 89 to loop around to Helena and on to Rimini, a speck on the map but hiding both a few old ghosts and Red Mountain. We never exactly found the ghost town part of Rimini, but had a great time hiking the Red Mountain trail; we came across a family of pheasants that let us get relatively close and found an old mining cabin which still held a few shards of pottery, long lost to the mud but poking up enough for us to find. The trail itself was a little more advanced than we expected; our legs were so tired on the way down that we got to giggling uncontrollably while trying to keep our balance. After our descent, we headed back into Helena for the Montana Power Summer Symphony, a big statewide event held outdoors on the campus of Carroll College. Members from all the symphonies in Montana joined together for a night of music and a general atmosphere of Montana camaraderie, all under a beautiful summer night sky. • **August 1999**

There are hundreds of moments I would relive from the years I lived in Montana — but for now, here are five from my last year. I loved living in this state; if there is ever a question about how I felt about it.

VARIATION: *Choose a specific year of your life, your best dates with your spouse before you were married, big milestones and transitions in your life, or memorable days you've spent with friends or family members. I chose five, but pick any number you want.*

Spokane with Susan and Suzanne

After a long and rewarding season of coaching speech and debate, Susan, Suzanne and I made plans for a road trip. The previous year we went to Billings to see *Stomp* but this year we decided to venture further. I cannot emphasize enough how much fun it was to do anything with these two. Sitting in an empty room would be fun with them—traveling to "the big city" for a long weekend of shopping, eating, and show-going was beyond fun. With Suzanne—a Gonzaga alumni—as our guide, we wandered around downtown stopping anywhere that looked interesting (the highlight, by far, was Auntie's Bookstore on W. Main St.). We ate anywhere that smelled good. We saw *Phantom of the Opera* at the Spokane Opera House. We slept late and took our time. Time is something teachers lack during the school year, but we managed to spend hours and hours doing exactly what we wanted to do: talk, laugh, and enjoy each other's company. • **March 2000**

To make this task more manageable, I limited the time frame to a specific year of my life: the last year I lived in Montana. Digging through photographs from that year was great fun as I struggled to choose just five days—there were so many more I could have included!

February 20

Ansel Adams's Birthday

"Twelve significant
photos in any one
year is a good crop."
—Ansel Adams

12 x 12 album

Swinging

Meadowridge Park
Colorado Springs, CO
May 25, 2006

This photo captures so much
about playgroup in Colorado;
Reagan and Maddie are absolutely
wrapped up in the joy of
swinging, not all all concerned
with anything other than the fun
of the moment. I'm not sure who
Reagan was smiling at—maybe no
one—but I love both their smiles.

Supergracie

East Legacy Dr
Mountain House, CA
October 1, 2006

Gracie loves almost nothing more than being thrown up in the air. This isn't the best photo in Baualda's portfolio but I think it's one of the album's best photos of Gracie because when you see her there on the photo I know where I'll be because it's her daddy catching her, and her smile tells us she's as free as can be.

Butterfly

Butterfly Pavilion
Denver, CO
May 12, 2005

The Butterfly Garden was small but we spent more than an hour circling around and around the perimeter in search of cool butterflies just trying to get a closer look. This was one of my favorites with so much green balanced by the dark of orange. I'm used to my favorites but this blur through on the son.

Pacific O.

Pescadero State Beach
Pescadero, CA
July 22, 2006

Mahoe, she saw the dramatic ocean as I'd seen her on the Pacific Ocean of it that she embodied by the waves and body in that same time with the most with its border of people to read she's setting no duty in that photo because every 10% of how and see at the waves as Baula's super it or maybe a position in it almost so it.

Karahalis Kids

Pescadero State Beach
Pescadero, CA
September 1, 2006

We had such a good time when the Karahalis family came to visit our Labor Day. I love trips to Pescadero we had the beach almost empty so somehow a rare water adventure in September and I felt I caught a change of clothes for they change, and Sam so we could have a photo shoot. This was my favorite shot of the Karahalis kid everyone through and through.

I'VE BEEN USING CAMERAS NEARLY ALL my life, but it wasn't until high school that I discovered the photography of Ansel Adams and understood the stark difference between taking a picture and making a photograph. While I don't expect to reach Adams-esque skill in my lifetime (or in any subsequent lifetime!), I m grateful for what his work has taught me: to be mindful of what I see through the lens of my camera.

"Twelve significant photographs in any one year is a good crop," Adams once said. It's ironic that such a prolific photographer would be the source of that freeing thought. With his words in mind, I created a book of 12 photographs significant to me for different reasons. It was difficult at first to narrow my selection to only 12, but I'm proud of the collection I gathered.

TIP: I've never used such large photos before, but I wanted to create a look that seemed more like a photography portfolio than an album, so I chose 8 x 12 (and 12 x 8) enlargements to achieve this goal. And you know what? I love these extra-large photos. It wouldn't be cost efficient to use this size all the time, but for an album of only 12, it was perfect. Check around for labs that will print a true 8 x 12 enlargement (I used scrapbookpictures.com), and you won't lose a single bit of print area in your photograph.

NATIONAL EATING DISORDERS AWARENESS
Week focuses on educating people about the dangers of
eating disorders and their impact on those battling them.

Scrapbooking is a fun hobby, but don't rule out its healing
potential for sensitive subject matter. Anna's decision to tell
the story of her struggle with anorexia was difficult and
emotionally exhausting, but she knew it would be worth it:
her children will have access to the full story of her life.

Crossroads

In July 1992, during Summer break we travelled to Toronto, Canada, via Washington DC so that Mum and Dad could set up their home for a year. This break also included a whirlwind vacation to Las Vegas, San Diego and Hollywood. I think it was the change of scene and feeling once again safe under my parents' protective wing that allowed me to start dating again. At this time I was free from responsibility and from the issues over which I had no control. I regarded weight. I think we were all lulled into a false sense of security.

On returning to High Pavement for my second and last year of A Levels, which is notoriously the most stressful year of any educational course, the control issue, or lack of, once again reared it's head. I was incredibly lonely and I just didn't fit in. Weekends were spent alone while everyone else was at home with family. For school breaks I was uprooted and flown to Canada, further increasing my awareness that I was different. I soon found that food once again became my solace. I can't remember when or how I started the binging and purging which is still to this day a very difficult for me to admit and talk about. I just remember what a vicious cycle it was: How I felt compelled to do it, like I had no choice, the huge release I felt after doing it, and then the intense feeling of shame. I had transitioned to Bulimia Nervosa.

I was like I drug. I am not stupid. I was always top of my class in school. I knew what I was doing was harmful, but I couldn't stop it. I tried again and again to stop but the more I failed, the more I did it, leading to even more shame which in turn led me to do it again and again. I was desperate to stop. This cycle continued. Though Bulimia does not have the physical manifestation of Anorexia, it is equally as harmful, almost more so, as the disorder is easier to conceal. My weight would stay the same so no-one knew that I had a problem. Over time, my hair started falling out, my muscles were fatigued, I was clearly depressed, my throat and esophagus were often sore (I was lucky not to rupture the latter), the skin on my knuckles was irritated, my period had stopped, and I didn't know it at the time, but my I was suffering from a loss of electrolytes. I was malnourished and was at high risk of heart failure.

Easter 1993, I became very sick with Pneumonia, so sick in fact that my Mum had to come back to the UK to attend college. It took me three months to recover and when I did it was only just in time to sit my A-Level exams. I don't know how I did it, but I came through with an A and two Bs. This meant I was accepted to the University of my choice. The pneumonia was the jolt I needed to stop. University was also a difficult time for me but I fumbled my way through it. Having had to grow up so quickly I really didn't fit in with the hoards of students who were getting their freedom for the first time. I honestly felt in limbo for most of the 4 years. College for me was just another "chapter"; A means of getting to the point where hopefully my life would finally begin. I remember walking to my classes each day, longing to join that rat race of 9amms, ters heading to work. I was depressed not hopeless.

My weight continued to be an issue and there were relapses, here and there, until Dec 1995, when I met the man who would change my life in more ways than I could ever have imagined. He respected me, he didn't judge me and more importantly he believed in the potential of the real me. I knew that within 2 days of meeting this guy, that he was the one I wanted to spend my life with.

toDay
i live in the quiet joyous expectation of good

afterword

And so, if you have got this far, it's likely you will not quite think of me in the same way as you did maybe 1/2 hour ago, and I am okay with that. After almost 32 years, I am finally comfortable enough in my own skin to be open and honest about who I am and how I got here. There is much truth in the popular saying that, life is a journey and not a destination. So far for me it has been quite a ride.

I need you to know that I am not perfect and never will be. I have issues just like everyone else, whether they choose to admit them or not. I am not proud of everything that has happened in my past but it is this very history that has shaped me to be the mother, wife and human being that I am today.

And you know what? If, in reading my story, you take just a small piece of it away with you, and learn from my experience, then I feel I will have succeeded, and I will honestly be able to say that it was all worthwhile.

I can live with any resulting loss of respect or whispering behind my back. "Sticks and stones may break my bones but names will never hurt me."

Please use your voice.

JULY MEMORIES
J '06

UNDERSTANDING annarexia

TIP: To stay organized, Anna gathers her digital papers and stamps into a folder on her computer before she starts designing. By repeating the same products in different arrangements, Anna achieved a diverse look in this photo book that's still cohesive—and much quicker than starting from scratch on every page. Anna's digital design secret? Just give yourself permission to play—don't over think the design.

8 x 8 photo book
by Anna Aspnes

Between Jan 21 – Feb 20

EVENT

Chinese New Year

Apples are a sign wealth.

Oranges and tangerines are a symbol of good health and long life. Tangerines with leaves intact are thought to ensure long lasting relationships and lots of children.

Noodles represent longevity but they should not be cut, and dropping your chopsticks is considered bad luck. Knives or scissors are avoided on New Year's Day as this may cut off fortune.

WHAT DO KUMQUATS, sunflowers, new clothes, and the color red all have in common? Each has a symbolic role in traditional Chinese New Year celebrations. Because her mother-in-law is Chinese, Anna's family observes Chinese New Year. She wanted her children, Ella and Luke, to have a basic understanding of what the holiday is all about. This simple board book album is the perfect teaching tool—it's easy for little hands to hold yet big enough to tell the story of an important family tradition.

TIP: *Don't adhere your page or photo edges too close to the hinges of your book or it will continually spring open.*

How will our children know who they are if they don't know where they come from?

John Steinbeck
(The Grapes of Wrath)

In the Far East, this is also the end of winter and the beginning of spring. Farmers take this opportunity to welcome spring as they plant for the new harvest. Thus, the Lunar New Year is also called the Spring Festival.

The entire house should be cleaned before New Year's Day. On New Year's Eve, all brooms, brushes are put away for fear that good fortune will be swept away.

All debts should be paid off for the New Year and it is unlucky to borrow or lend money during this time. Red envelopes called "Lai Sees" containing crisp bank notes are exchanged as a sign of good fortune.

5 x 5 mini-album
by Anna Aspnes

February 26

Johnny Cash's

Birthday

"you build
on failure
you use it
as a
stepping
stone
close the
door on the
past, you
don't try to
forget the
mistakes,
but you
don't dwell
on it, you
don't let it
have any
of your
energy, or
any of your
time, or
any of your
space."
j. cash

B brendan, age five
with pop pop in connecticut

11 x 8½ page
by Laura Kurz

JOHNNY CASH IS A LEGENDARY AMERICAN MUSICIAN, one who sold more than 50 million albums in a career spanning almost 50 years. His life and music were filled with recklessness, sorrow, joy, creativity, love, and the power of redemption. If you've never spent time listening to his music and lyrics, give it a try—you could create hundreds of pages inspired by his life and songs. Or, think of a music idol of your own, and make a layout about his or her influence on your life.

Combining a quote by Johnny Cash with this old photo of her brother and grandfather, Laura acknowledges the difficulties her brother has experienced while still holding out hope for the future. Her simple, striking design keeps the focus on her poignant photo.

"You build on failure. You use it as a stepping stone. Close the door on the past. You don't try to forget the mistakes; but you don't dwell on it. You don't let it have any of your energy, or any of your time, or any of your space." **Johnny Cash**

1
2
3
4
5
6
7
8
9
10
11
12
13
14
15
16
17
18
19
20
21
22
23
24
25
26
27
28
29
30
31

This month...

honor the women who came before you

make a creative mess with a child

make something with your hands

be proud of your name

grab some popcorn and enjoy the show

rescue your childhood mementos from an ugly shoebox

get to know your brain

document a family passion

write a letter to an incredible kid

what's your name ?

gabriel

michelle

gabriella

owen

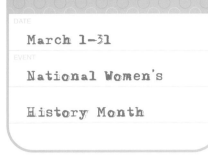

8 x 4 handmade album

WHEN YOU THINK ABOUT WOMEN'S HISTORY, who comes to mind? Eleanor Roosevelt? Marie Curie? Amelia Earhart? These are the women I remember most from my elementary school history lessons. There are other women in history worthy of your attention, though—the women who came before you in your family tree. Spend some time this month thinking about these grandmothers, mothers, aunts, and sisters. Their history is your history.

Until a few years ago, I knew nothing about Daddy's paternal side of the family; he knew very little either, but recent contact with a few long-lost cousins has provided us with new, treasured information. This photo from 1907 of my great-grandmother Grace Mabel Folsom Willis and her family is the only real tangible evidence I have of her life as a young woman—she is approximately 31 in this picture, while my great-grandfather Frank is 43. They would eventually have ten children; pictured here are Madison, Norton, Joseph, twins Frank and Maxine, and William. My grandfather Thomas was the youngest of the ten, born in 1915. I want to ask her: How in the world were you able to keep up with all those mischievous looking children? Did you have a place you could go for a little quiet?

This photo of the Walton girls is one of my favorite old photos. I wish we knew exactly what year it was taken; sometime between 1895–1900 is our best guess. Lillian Walton (either the first or fourth from left to right) was born in November 1865, the fourth of six girls. By the time she was 34 she would have four children: Sylvia (1891), Alice (1894), Austa (1896), and Marian (1900). She would have two more—Howard (1903) and Marie, my grandma, in 1907. It was difficult to have so many girls when they needed boys to work the farm. I want to ask her: What kind of relationship did your daughters have with all your sisters? Were people surprised at the sheer amount of women in your family?

One of the driving forces behind my scrapbooking is a curiosity for what my ancestors felt about the universal human experiences we share. I wish I could ask them how they handled parenting, managing a household, and their educational or occupational pursuits; I wish I could listen to their funny, frustrating or joyous life stories. I made this little album to remind me that my grandmothers were once the same age that I am now (34), and that I'm part of a rich history of interesting women.

Hazel Mae, Grandma Rinehart's mother and my Nana, was born in 1895. She married Harry Anderson and when she was 23 in 1918, had Grandma and a twin who died at birth. Helen was born eight years later in 1926. From what I can tell, Hazel was about 34 in this family photograph; Helen looks approximately three years old by height. The Anderson family lived in Berwyn, Illinois in 1929. I want to ask her: What did you do with Grandma and Aunt Helen for fun when they were this age? What was Grandma like as a little girl? Was she a lot like Gracie—full of energy and life and rough and tumble?

Oh, how I love this photograph of Grandma Watson dressed in white. Born in 1907, Grandma (Marie Lillian) was the youngest of six children. This photo was probably taken at a school picnic before she left teaching to have children; like me, she taught for a number of years first. She was 32 when Ron was born in 1939 and at 34, was pregnant with Mama. I want to ask her: What was it like to be pregnant for you? Did you have aches and pains? Did you have to remind yourself to drink enough water?

March 1-31

Youth Art Month

THE COUNCIL FOR ART Education has designated March as Youth Art Month in an effort to promote the value of art education for kids. I believe a sense of accomplishment is instilled in children who get to be artistic: they realize they have the power to create something by themselves, when most of their world is created or managed for them.

Before our girls were in preschool, my neighbor Melissa and I hatched a plan to make art a more regular part of our lives—and Art Friday, a bi-weekly, hour-and-a-half crafting session, was born. All you need to get started are some basic supplies and a few project ideas from magazines or your own imagination. Document these sessions and create visual reminders that creativity is valued in your house.

NOTE: Like all the best art projects, I made this one up as I went along. Cork board? I found it when I was looking for a different material to use, and I thought "why not?" It's fun to improvise—try it, you'll see.

art friday

what will we do today?

12 x 20 wall hanging

DATE

March 1-31

EVENT

National Craft Month

IF YOU'RE A SCRAPBOOKER, CHANCES ARE you also harbor a deep appreciation for other crafty pursuits. National Craft Month gives you a chance to celebrate all of your creative endeavors—from quilting to beading to felt-animal making, and everything in between.

my every crafting endeavor is a fervent effort to leave

traces of love in ink, paper, or stitches.

8½ x 11 page
by Mi'Chelle Larsen

Mi'Chelle is a crafty woman, always fashioning something out of paper or ribbon or fabric, and her work is always heartfelt and beautiful. But instead of focusing on the projects she creates, this simple layout conveys her personal philosophy about crafting. Have you ever thought about why you make things with your hands? I bet someone, someday, would love to know. Tell them now.

NAMES MATTER. HOW ELSE CAN YOU ACCOUNT for the thousands of name books available for parents-to-be? As Sigmund Freud said, "a human being's name is a principal component in his person, perhaps a piece of his soul." The goal of Celebrate Your Name Week is straightforward: a name is an identity, and celebrating that name boosts self-confidence, pride, and individuality.

Mi'Chelle was drawn to (read: obsessed with) the art of naming because of her own unique name. As a collector of name books, it seemed only natural to create a little guide to her family's names: how they were chosen, what they mean, how they are shortened, and how popular (or rare) they are.

TIP: *When using transparencies or overlays in an album, try sewing your photo or patterned paper onto them to avoid glue show-through.*

We wanted you to have something to live up to, so we named

owen
thomas
larsen

owen. Be like them.

owen

hickname : OWEO

meaning : young warrior; of noble birth

ranking : **60**

YOU WERE ALMOST : Anders Macfarlane

We wanted you to have something to live up to, so we named you after two of the finest men we knew -- Momma's great-grandpa Owen Olsen and Daddy's grandpa Martin Thomas. Both men who knew what it meant to walk uprightly before God. Learn about them, Owen. Be like them.

owen

4 x 6 mini-album
by Mi'Chelle Larsen

DATE

Variable, March

EVENT

The Oscars/Academy Awards

THE ACADEMY OF MOTION PICTURE ARTS and Sciences was created in 1927. Today it has more than 6,000 filmmakers who work tirelessly to advance excellence in movies. Each year the awards handed out by The Academy create a worldwide buzz about movies, actors, and the glamour of Hollywood. It's a great time of year to reflect on the movies you love, whether they're award-worthy or not.

Any Given Wednesday

007817 104965

Take an ordinary night of the week. Add a bowl of microwave popcorn, an ice cold Pepsi, a jumbo bag of Strawberry Twizzlers. Select the most entertaining DVD you can find at Blockbuster, and you have "Any Given Wednesday." Inspired by the true story of a young husband and wife trying to make quality time for each other. Derrick MacAskill is the easy-going husband who enjoys a riveting drama, while his adoring wife (Mary MacAskill) would rather laugh along with a romantic comedy. Whatever the genre, join Derrick and Mary as they cozy up on the couch for 120 minutes of unfettered entertainment!

DATE NIGHT presents AN ORDINARY WEEKDAY production A MACASKILL TRADITION film
"ANY GIVEN WEDNESDAY" starring DERRICK MACASKILL MARY MACASKILL
popcorn ORVILLE REDENBACHER drink PEPSI CO., INC. candy HERSHEY'S TWIZZLERS STRAWBERRY TWISTS
© 2007 DATE NIGHT. ALL RIGHTS RESERVED.

APPROX. RUNNING TIME 160 MINUTES
PRINTED IN CANADA

© Layout and Design Mary MacAskill. All rights reserved. Design can be copied with written permission and small fee of milk chocolate, preferably Twix, King size. Page completed for entertainment purposes only.

12 x 12 page
by Mary MacAskill

Mary and her husband Derrick love movies so much that they have a standing date on Wednesday nights to rent a DVD and enjoy traditional movie fare (i.e., eat popcorn for dinner) in the comfort of their living room. What better way to celebrate your love for movies than by drawing on movie packaging for your design inspiration, as Mary did here?

DATE

March 12

EVENT

Girl Scout Founding

Day Anniversary

8 x 10 covered keepsake box

JULIETTE GORDON LOW FOUNDED the American Girl Guides—later changed to Girl Scouts—on March 12, 1912, with a group of 18 girls in Savannah, Georgia. Since that time, millions of girls worldwide have benefited from the principles, activities, and friendships found within Girl Scouts. Today, Girl Scouts seeks to "change the way girls see their world and their place in it." When you think about it, that's the goal of scrapbooking, too!

As a former Girl Scout, I have some treasured scouting items that have been stored in an unremarkable old shoebox for years. I decided some time ago that I wanted to create a more worthy home for my hard-earned badges and other materials, but it wasn't until K & Company partnered with Girl Scouts of the USA to create a line of scrapbooking papers and embellishments that I knew what I would do with everything. A box lover through and through, I decided to customize a box to hold my mementos. Sure, my things went from one box to another, but I think the second one is much cuter. Displayable, even. Best of all? I was able to finish the project in just under an hour.

Mid-March

Brain Awareness Week

8 x 8 photo book
by Anna Aspnes

IS THERE ANYTHING MORE MYSTERIOUS THAN the workings of the human brain? The Dana Alliance for Brain Initiatives actually strives to make the brain a little less mysterious by advancing public awareness about all varieties of brain research, especially through Brain Awareness Week. While the brain might seem an odd theme for a scrapbook at first glance, there are countless topics to cover.

Anna chose a particularly serious issue—depression—as subject matter for her Brain Awareness Week album. Anna's own battle with depression is both intensely personal and extremely important to share. Because children of a depressed parent have a higher risk of depression themselves, Anna wanted to put an end to the silence and stigma of her own experience and provide a means for discussing the condition with her children in an open and visual way. This simple photo book fit the bill perfectly.

TIP: *Anna loves the professional finish of Shutterfly's photo books. Their slim profile allows her to place more of them on a bookshelf, and letting someone else do the printing gives her more time to do the creating.*

Which came first?
Eating Disorder or Depression
It's the classic chicken/egg paradox

as SOME pursue HAPPINESS others "CREATE iT"

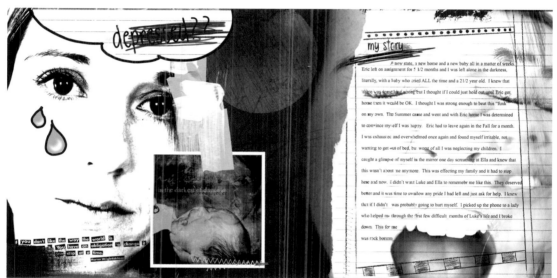

depressed??

my story

A new state, a new home and a new baby all in a matter of weeks. Eric left on assignment for 5 1/2 months and I was left alone in the darkness, literally, with a baby who cried ALL the time and a 2 1/2 year old. I knew that there was something wrong but I thought if I could just hold out until Eric got home then it would be OK. I thought I was strong enough to beat this "funk" on my own. The Summer came and went and with Eric home I was determined to convince myself I was happy. Eric had to leave again in the Fall for a month. I was exhausted and overwhelmed once again and found myself irritable, not wanting to get out of bed, but worst of all I was neglecting my children. I caught a glimpse of myself in the mirror one day screaming at Ella and knew that this wasn't about me anymore. This was effecting my family and it had to stop here and now. I didn't want Luke and Ella to remember me like this. They deserved better and it was time to swallow any pride I had left and just ask for help. I knew that if I didn't I was probably going to hurt myself. I picked up the phone to a lady who helped me through the first few difficult months of Luke's life and I broke down. This for me was rock bottom.

"THE UNIVERSE IS FULL OF MAGICAL THINGS patiently waiting FOR OUR WITS TO GROW SHARPER" eden phillpotts

My Happy Pills

I have always been one to "Say No" to drugs, both recreational and medicinal, so it took a little persuasion and I think sheer desperation to finally convince me to give them a shot. My doctor prescribed me with Zoloft because I was still feeding Luke, and told me "I would soon be seeing the world in color again". She was right. I would not be without these babies now. I am lucky to be one of the 35-45% of people who can be treated with antidepressants. They have made such a huge difference to my life. I am happier, less volatile and more at ease with myself. I definitely choose personal happiness over the stigma of taking antidepressants.

Wheresoever you go, go with all your heart. Confucius

During the NCAA Basketball Tournament

March Madness

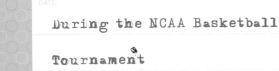

EACH MARCH IT HAPPENS. TYPICALLY mild-mannered folks become rabid basketball aficionados, clutching funny pieces of paper they call "brackets" like they're winning lottery tickets. What's going on here? A common case of March Madness, caused by the excitement of 65 college basketball teams vying for the national championship. Exciting stuff.

Each year as the symptoms of March Madness emerge, my family springs to action. Yahoo groups are created, email messages are exchanged, and predictions are made about who will win, who will lose, and who will be smart enough to guess it all.

Some of the funniest things my family says all year are declared in March, so I decided to collect them all and create a record of the hoopla. I saw this as a rare opportunity to add the words of family members who don't normally write to the "permanent record." I guarantee that this album will be pulled out at family gatherings for years to come as we fondly remember the craziness we experience during March Madness.

VARIATION: *Don't care about basketball?—No problem! Let this album inspire you to record your loved ones' thoughts about a hobby or passion shared by your family.*

reason
no.243
That I love my family:
they are really funny
during the NCAA
basketball tournament

This is Great!
posted by Ben (Asst. Manager Roundball)
March 14, 2007

We have poets and preachers, mothers and teachers;
Trojans and Bruins, oh my.

Once this gets started, you will have no control but to
watch the momentum rumble and tumble like a kid on a
bike going down a big grassy hill. His feet will leave the
pedals, as they spin much too fast.

"Hold on, hold on, hold on" you will find yourself in a
mumbled chant.
Your team is ahead, "Hold on"
Your team is behind, "Hold on"
There are moments left, a huddled time-out, a dry erase
clipboard.
A pass, a dribble, a slippery grip on a round object, "Hold
on" you will yell. They can't hear you. The ball is in the
air...

Now, Matt....
posted by Katherine (Orange Seed)
March 17, 2007

You are understandably disappointed by your mediocre
showing. But is it really necessary to pick on my poor
sweet sister? After all, her pick name simply states the
facts. Consider it an honor that she chose to wave the
banner bearing your name; she could have easily called
herself "I Beat Library Bookie Last Year" or even "I Beat
The People For Whom Technical Difficulties Prevented
the Full Completion of Their Brackets Last Year." But
she didn't. She chose you. It's like a big March Madness
hug, just for you.

It's still early. I'm hoping that my decision to send
Vanderbilt to the Final Four (based, of course, on the
fact that they have a wonderful Divinity School) pays off.
For one who normally does not follow sports, I was a
raving lunatic during Overtime(s).

4 x 7¾ spiral album

DATE
Third Thursday in March

EVENT
Absolutely Incredible

Kid Day

November 2006

Dear Laurel,

While you've only met me
once in your first year of life,
I feel as though I can say with some
authority that you are one incredible kid.
I've known your parents, your Grandma Bunny,
your Grandpa Jake, and your Uncle Steve
for more than ten years now and I know
how happy your long-awaited birth made
them. They are believers in the most
important things in life, and already
they are passing those principles and
passions on to you. Your mama and daddy
share your photos all the time, and it's
easy to see your great sense of security
and happiness—feelings that lead to
great things, thoughts, and actions. You
possess an indomitable streak, one that will
serve you well as you discover
what the world has to offer you,
and what you have to offer the
world. You are bound for big
things, sweet Laurel Rose.
Love, Elizabeth

incredibly happy.

12 x 12 page

CAMP FIRE USA'S GOAL IS FOR ALL children in America to receive a letter on Absolutely Incredible Kid Day communicating how valuable they are. As the organization states, research shows "that simple words of encouragement and compassion can make a difference in a child's life. Putting those words into a letter allows the recipient to hang onto those encouraging words, and return to them for inspiration and guidance...." Why stop there, though? Turn your letter into a scrapbook page and give it away.

It's really quite easy to create a scrapbook page to honor this unique observance. I chose a picture of Laurel, an incredible kid indeed, and paired it with a handwritten letter and a few simple embellishments. Laurel won't be able to read her letter for some time, but it's still a permanent reminder of how much she is loved!

TIP: Handwrite your letter. Trust me, no child who receives a letter (or scrapbook page) is going to criticize the handwriting of the grownup that happily surprised her. It only makes it more special!

April

1
2
3
4
5
6
7
8
9
10
11
12

This month...

13

invite poetry onto your pages — 14

be an advocate for understanding — 15

let your imagination take flight — 16

play ball! — 17

get inspired by every bloomin' thing — 18

be kind to the earth — 19

share a story, save a cent — 20

plant a tree and watch respect grow — 21

22
23
24
25
26
27
28
29
30

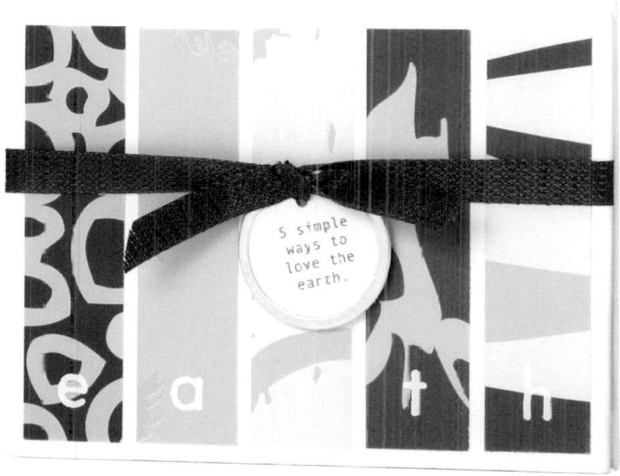
5 simple ways to love the earth.
e
a
t
h

April 1-30

National Poetry Month

EVERY YEAR SINCE 1996 THE Academy of American Poets has sponsored National Poetry Month, a month-long observance to draw attention to the value of poetry in our society.

I'm drawn to poetry because I love the depth of emotion and perspective that can be communicated in so few words. I love how a single line can sum up everything I feel. I believe that you can tell a lot about a person by examining the books she reads and the poetry she loves. For this reason I decided to create an album with 12 of my favorite poems, one for each month of the year. I paired my chosen verses with a beloved photo and memory, keeping the same design scheme for each page and varying only the background patterned paper. This album is different from anything I've ever made, and it's inspiring me to revisit my long-lost hobby of memorizing favorite poems.

11 x 8½ album

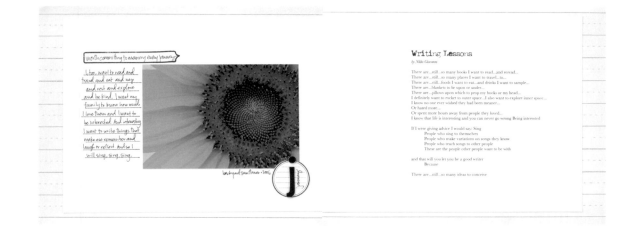

This Is Aunt Luella

I was sitting at my computer in my classroom at Great Falls High when I got the email from D with the news that Great-Great Aunt Luella had died. I never knew her particularly well—had last seen her 15 years or more before, but I remember her as a friendly woman who loved to make things and lived for the Chicago Bears. Katherine looks so much like her and the poem she wrote is my favorite she's ever written.

Aunt Luella in Chicago

february

Aunt Luella was Dreaming of a Dried-Flower Mosaic
2.3.00

by Katherine E. W. Pershey

I met Aunt Luella just once,
in Chicago. I don't remember why
we went. She called me
"Doll" and buttered my rye
for me at dinner. Her house
was filled with artwork,
not the kind you try not
to look at—things that were
quietly beautiful, trinkets she
made herself when her fingers
were still young. She painted
delicate flowers onto saucers
and carved families
out of dried apples.
She loved football
and my grandmother,
who is in Mexico and
does not know that
Aunt Luella died this morning.
She was sleeping, musing
of spring and how when the
marigolds bloomed, she would
press them carefully in her
leather-bound book of Psalms.

Paul is happiest outdoors: feeling the crunch of leaves, walking to see a neighborhood Japanese fish pond, running up and down hills, running in grass, running down the sidewalk with his daddy, playing in mud, picking fruit, riding in a wagon, picnics in the park, sliding down the bumpy slide at the park.

Just as children without autism, children with autism are unique. Some, like Paul, love the outdoors; others cannot tolerate the sensory overload.

I love to pick apples and blueberries at the farm with my family.

AUTISM IS A NEUROLOGICAL DISORDER that affects 1 in 150 children born in the United States; because it is characterized as a spectrum disorder, symptoms vary in severity. While scientists cannot explain the cause of autism, research has found many new answers in recent years about the condition, intervention, and treatment.

I once read that many parents of autistic children are generally so exhausted at the end of each day that they simply don't have the energy to advocate for more research, funding, or awareness in the quest to understand and cure autism. My friend Linda and her husband know this exhaustion firsthand, living daily with their son Paul's severe autism. I've always wanted to help them somehow—to bring them dinner, to run errands, to simply be an understanding physical presence—but we've lived on opposite ends of the country for years. Then it occurred to me that, as a scrapbooker, I could create an album about Paul that might double as a teaching tool for Paul's younger relatives or even local community members at their public library or synagogue. I chose a simple board book format, sturdy enough for little hands to hold and colorful enough to hold the interest of young eyes. I asked Linda for photos and two lists: things Paul likes and things he dislikes. The result is a glimpse of Paul's life in which he is simply Paul, not Paul Who Has Autism.

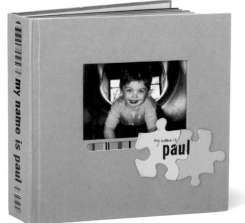

6½ x 6½ mini-album

Paul loves water: drinking water, pouring water out of cups, watching water fall, playing in the rain, swimming in Vermont lake water, watching the water fountain at the park, splashing at the water park or in the ocean, playing with water toys or sprinklers.

Water play is often used as a teaching and therapy tool with autistic children.

Almost nothing is better than splashing in the water on a sunny day.

Paul is affectionate: he loves tickles, kisses and hugs, and can ask for piggy back rides from his teacher and daddy. He cannot express his feelings with words as other children his age might be able to, but can point, listen, and use some sign language to be understood.

It is a myth that autistic children are unable to show affection. Many autistic children smile, look at others in the eye, give and receive physical affection, and develop friendships and relationships with others.

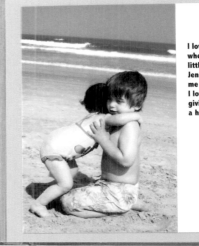

I love when my little sister Jenna gives me a kiss. I love giving her a hug.

In 2007, the CDC states that 1 in 150 American children will be diagnosed with autism.

I am an autistic child.

I am unique.

My name is Paul.

DATE

April 1-30

EVENT

National Kite Month

DID YOU KNOW THAT KITES HAVE been around for more than 2,000 years? (The first recorded kite flight was in China in 200 B.C.) National Kite Month is a month-long celebration co-founded by the Kite Trade Association International and the American Kitefliers Association, designed to acquaint people with the rich and rewarding tradition of kite making and kite flying.

11 x 8½ page
by Margaret
Scarbrough

pull

Dexter Drumlin. Quite possibly the perfect location to fly a kite...*especially for the first time.* You were so excited to learn how to fly a kite, Matthew. So much so that you insisted on helping ah-pah build the kite...grabbing the instructions from him and trying to decipher the strange letters and diagrams. Too funny to watch. Of course the only thing you did was delay the kite-making process by a few minutes or so...but hey, it's the experience you were after, right? And what an experience it was. You absolutely loved it...every single minute. And I loved watching the both of you enjoy a perfect kite flying afternoon together.

Spring 2004

Have you seen a more perfect place to fly a kite than Dexter Drumlin, the lush meadow in Lancaster, Massachusetts, where Margaret's son Matthew first learned to fly a kite? Margaret wanted to make sure the beautiful color photos didn't clash with other elements on the page, so she chose a basic black-and-white combination with just a splash of color here and there, allowing her photos to shine.

DATE
First Monday in April

EVENT
Opening Day

on being a cleveland indians fan

it means that one of your earliest childhood memories is going to Cleveland Stadium to see an Indians vs. Yankees game in your favorite Indians halter top. That you harbor a demented hope, just like Doris Kearns Goodwin. That a perfect season is possible after a win on opening day. That you will actually cry when they lose the World Series in the 9th inning of the 7th game in 1997. That you will cry again when your cousin Dorothy dies in her old age and her obituary reads that she loved her family, writing, and the Cleveland Indians. That you will take your first-born child to her first game before she turns two months old. That you will teach your children to love the Indians before they learn the alphabet. That you will actually miss players who are traded, like Omar & Manny, in a way you miss friends who move away. That you never, ever give up hope that this is their year. April 2007

Maddie's first game July 2002

12 x 12 page

OPENING DAY DOESN'T JUST SIGNIFY the beginning of a new baseball season but the dawning of spring itself—a time full of hope and renewal, where anything is possible (including a World Series victory in October)

Yep, you guessed it—I'm one of "those" people. My love of baseball is a shared one, passed down for generations by like-minded relatives. Specifically, my family has the luck (or is it a curse?) of being Cleveland Indians fans, with all that implies: unshaken optimism and loyalty in the face of improbability year after year. I wanted to document this important part of my family's psyche—the part that truly believes that *this* is the year—because it's something that unites us. Maybe baseball isn't big in your family, and that's OK (weird, but OK), so spend a little time thinking about what does unite and define you instead.

DATE

Second week of April

EVENT

National Garden Week

IT ONLY MAKES SENSE THAT NATIONAL Gardening Week would be celebrated in April, a month full of observances meant to protect, improve, and beautify our earth. The mission of National Garden Week is to promote interest in one of the fastest growing hobbies in the United States—a hobby that seeks to add beauty, promote a healthy lifestyle, and advocate the importance of a balanced ecology.

Tucked along the stone pathways, spilling lazily from hanging pots, treading water in ponds. Velvety petals of cotton white, butter yellow, pale purple, flushed pink, raspberry red enveloped in skirts of waxy green. Color bursting from the grass. Daisies, lilies, roses, geraniums, peonies, begonias, dahlias. Flowers, flowers, flowers. Thousands of flowers. All in one place. All at the Butchart Gardens.

Our guidebook read, "the gardens...display more than a million plants throughout the year. As impressive as the numbers is the sheer perfection of each garden – not a blade out of place, each flower the same height, all blooming at the same time."

And a person can't forget the ivy-covered walkway in the Rose Garden, the ponds swimming with Koi, the curved red bridges of the Japanese Garden, the tranquil view of the ocean through the pine trees. Definitely a place to visit more than once.

12 x 12 spread
by Mary MacAskill

One of the best ways to celebrate National Garden Week is to immerse your senses in a lush, flowering garden as Mary did during her visit to Butchart Gardens in British Columbia, Canada. Mary was inspired by the glorious colors of the gardens, and when it came time to scrapbook her visit, she was thrilled to find patterned paper that matched so perfectly. A trip to a botanical garden can do wonders for your creativity: all that color and life is awe-inspiring!

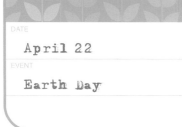

DATE

April 22

EVENT

Earth Day

Apr

6 x 4¼ mini-album
by Margaret Scarbrough

EARTH DAY WAS FOUNDED IN April 1970 as a grassroots effort to increase awareness of environmental issues. The first year saw 20 million people participate in Earth Day activities. The success and momentum caused by this first celebration led to the passing of the Clean Air Act and the creation of the Environmental Protection Agency.

Margaret designed her Earth Day mini-album to teach her sons to value the world around them and always leave it in better shape than they found it. She tailored her "earth" lessons to a level that they'll be able to understand, helping them learn earth-friendly habits from an early age.

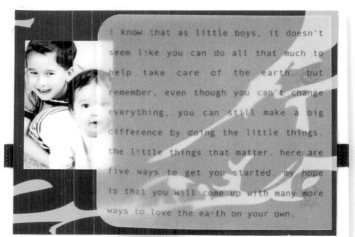

i know that as little boys, it doesn't seem like you can do all that much to help take care of the earth. but remember, even though you can't change everything, you can still make a big difference by doing the little things. the little things that matter. here are five ways to get you started. my hope is that you will come up with many more ways to love the earth on your own.

no. 1
reduce, reuse & recycle. this is a great way to start. make less of an impact on the earth. try drinking from a glass versus a juice box. or drawing on both sides of the paper.

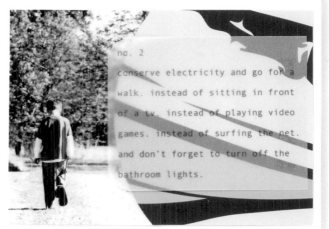

no. 2
conserve electricity and go for a walk. instead of sitting in front of a tv. instead of playing video games. instead of surfing the net. and don't forget to turn off the bathroom lights.

no. 3
get your hands dirty and plant a tree. water it. tend to it and watch it grow. soon enough, you will learn to love that tree. and have a greater concern for all living things as well.

61

EACH APRIL, MEMBERS OF THE American Bankers Association plan hundreds of presentations for children nationwide in an attempt to build financial literacy at a young age. Since the first Teach Children To Save Day, nearly 2 million children have learned essential lessons about how to save and spend money.

Anna created this page about the woman who taught her to save her money: her Grandma Day. Her explanation of saving money is not just practical advice, it's also home-grown wisdom shared across generations of Anna's family. What lessons (financial or otherwise) have your grandparents taught you that can be summed up on a scrapbook page?

12 x 12 page
by Anna Aspnes

TIP: *To create her coin background, Anna spread loose change across an inexpensive piece of white foam board, then stood by the window and took photos to provide context and emphasis for her message.*

DATE

Last Friday in April

EVENT

Arbor Day

ARBOR DAY WAS FIRST OBSERVED IN 1872 after J. Sterling Morton, a pioneer from Detroit, settled in the treeless plains of Nebraska. As a lover of nature and a journalist, Morton spread the word about the importance of planting trees, stressing how they both beautify the landscape and offer protection from the sun and wind.

The true meaning of life is to plant trees, under whose shade you do not expect to sit.

—Nelson Henderson

Maddie— if this is true, you are well on your way to figuring life out. [our precious hawthorn tree, planted in 2004 • Colorado Springs, CO]

12 x 12 page

As a family, we plant a tree or two every place we live. We believe respect for nature originates from helping outdoors, and we want our daughters to care about the environment. Matt and I love this photo of Maddie studying a tree intently as she waters it. Paired with the quote, it communicates a bit of family philosophy that we whole-heartedly support. Scrapbooks aren't just for memories— they can also communicate what a family stands for.

1
2
3
4
5
6
7
8
9
10
11
12
13
14
15
16
17
18
19
20
21
22
23
24
25
26
27
28
29
30
31

This month...

enjoy the ride

recount the drama of a move

reminisce about sporting days

catch someone with a book

honor a teacher

let a goose guide your design

be amazed at scrapbooking's gifts

remember those who have served

look to the low shelves for inspiration

revel in the diversity of the world

THE LEAGUE OF AMERICAN BICYCLISTS INITIATED National Bike Month in 1956 to promote bicycling for fun, fitness, and transportation—and to advocate a more bicycle-friendly America. Targeting the nation's 57 million cyclists, the organization sponsors a national Bike to Work Week and Bike to Work Day, both in May. On its website, the organization suggests 50 unique ways to celebrate National Bike Month, including "Plan a cycling vacation" and "Put on a bike rodeo at your kid's school."

I had a blast creating this little album charting Maddie's progression from new tricycle owner to proud tricycle graduate. I didn't have this album in mind when we gave Maddie her shiny red trike for her second birthday, but I later realized I had taken photographs every six months or so of her riding it on our basketball court. The book is simple. Each page includes a photograph and an appropriate quote about childhood or trikes, and I added little notes about her love of riding throughout. The bright colors and design of the Danny O mini-album filled in the rest.

6 x 6 mini-album

The best way to make children good is to make them happy

—Oscar Wilde

your shiny, red tricycle

Your first tricycle was a retro red Radio Flyer that Daddy and I found at Target after much searching, your big birthday gift for your second birthday. You loved it from the first moment you saw it. It didn't take long before you decided that riding your bike in the court was just about your favorite activity ever. Over the course of two years you put miles and miles on this tricycle— excited to ride in big circles with Kaity & Belle or content to ride alone, imagining adventures and "rides" to the library or post office. You traded in your trusty tricycle for a purple princess bike on your 4th birthday.

DID YOU KNOW THAT ABOUT 15 PERCENT OF THE U.S. population relocates each year? (Our family is definitely part of that percentage most years!) To educate people about what it takes to move from one home to the next, a moving company dubbed May as National Moving Month.

To Maddie & Gracie, our little move monkeys ♡ Mama & Da

a day-by-day (for better or worse) account ☺

6 x 6 mini-album

Since we live a somewhat transient lifestyle (due to Matt's military career), we are no strangers to the struggles of moving. If we've learned one thing, it's that you cannot box up your sense of humor—it needs to come along with you each step of the way. Before Matt's transfer from Colorado to a base in California, I decided to document our family's move, taking photos and keeping a written record of each day. While it isn't feasible for me to keep up a daily record of my life, this mini-album has a certain authenticity because the journaling was written in the moment.

June 12, 2006

Mama's Got a Lot of Scrapbook Supplies

And books.

And framed art.

As the packers pointed out multiple times over the past two days.

June 19, 2006

On the Road

Here we are, taking a little break at a rest stop in Parachute, CO. It was a good decision to drive I-70 W instead of I-80. Wow. There is some truly beautiful country in Colorado.

[Later in the evening]

So What Did You Do Tonight?

I just got back from cruising the strip in Green River, Utah; population not very many.

With Gracie.

In our pajamas.

Because getting her to go to bed in a one-room hotel room is so much fun. But wait! There's more!

Maddie, who earlier told us she's allergic to the pizza she ate, made good on her promise and threw it all up all over everywhere. I can't tell you how much I didn't enjoy scrubbing a bed, bathroom, and hotel carpet in the near-dark so as not to wake Gracie, sleeping one foot away from the scene of the crime. The oh-so-helpful night manager at the desk suggested we keep all the towels in the room for housekeeping to pick up in the morning, to which I politely said no, while thinking very impolite things.

She may win best traveler award on this trip. We'll see.

May 25, 2006

Buried

No matter how good a job you think you do at pre-packing before a military move, it becomes apparent very quickly that you DIDN'T.

No matter how badly you wish that your furniture will look nice and new and cared for when it comes off the truck, it DOESN'T.

No matter how friendly your packers were while they put your most treasured things in boxes, they will still do a crummy job and things will be BROKEN.

No matter how hard you work all day unpacking box after box after box, there will be ANOTHER BOX.

No matter how much bigger your new house is than your old house, there still doesn't seem to be room enough for your possessions (the ones you THOUGHT you pared down so carefully before it all started).

We're looking for the light at the end of the tunnel... it's there, we know... this is the fourth time we've done this in 11 years. Grandma Poppins is here helping care for monkeys, and we're working pretty much nonstop to get it all done by the time she leaves. Wish us luck.

DATE

May 1–31

EVENT

National Physical Fitness and Sports Month

MAY IS THE PERFECT TIME TO think about physical fitness: spring is in full bloom and summer is just around the corner. The U.S. Government thinks so, too. Since 1983, May has been observed as National Physical Fitness and Sports Month, with the mission of encouraging all Americans to move more, live healthier lives, and recognize the value of sports.

Laura was inspired by this observance to celebrate a piece of her sporty past: for nine years, she was a competitive figure skater. After collecting the photos she has of herself skating, she created a small mini-album from scratch using a very simple color and design scheme to put it all together. It's easier than you think to make a unique theme album, especially if you have a limited number of photos to work with—simply create as many pages as you can fill with photos and memories! Laura's design incorporates cardstock, patterned paper, and a spare post from a larger post-bound album to hinge it all together. Be careful, though: designing your own mini-albums can be highly addicting! Consider yourself warned.

5 x 2½ mini-album
by Laura Kurz

DATE

May 1-31

EVENT

Get Caught

Reading Month

WHAT DO FIRST LADY LAURA BUSH, YODA THE Jedi master, Queen Latifah, Donald Duck, and my daughter Maddie have in common? They've all been caught reading, and there are photos* to prove it. The Association of American Publishers sponsors Get Caught Reading Month each May as a way to encourage young people to pick up a book and get lost in the story.

11 x 8½ page

This is one of my favorite baby photos of you, Maddie. Even though I can't see your face, this captures so much of your emerging personality. I had just peeked in your room to see if you were still taking your morning nap, and I found you quietly looking at one of our favorite books. I ran, on tiptoe, to grab my camera and catch you. I was so lucky to make it back without disturbing you. photo taken March 2003/10 months

FROM THE LIBRARY OF Madeline Hazel

*Visit getcaughtreading.org to download or order a poster of each of these personalities (except Maddie) with their noses stuck in a book.

If you haven't guessed it by now, books are a pretty big deal at our house. Everywhere you look, we've got shelves, baskets, nightstands, and (most of the time) a kitchen counter overflowing with books. It isn't too hard to get caught reading there! One of my favorite photos of all-time is this shot of Maddie all snuggled up in her crib with a Sandra Boynton classic, *But Not the Hippopotamus.* Even if you don't "catch" someone in your family reading this month, make sure to steal a photograph or two of a loved one engrossed in an activity she loves. Not all photographs need to be filed with a smiling face. Candid shots often express more than a posed photo could hope to convey.

Room 218

In six years of teaching, I taught in a total of nine classrooms. But my room will always be Room 218. It was the room at the end of the hallway next to the Old Gym, the room with the Narnia chair (where you could pretend you were in Narnia by looking out the window at the lamp post on a snowy day), the room with the huge debate cabinets, the room with the beautiful oak desk and chair that I could hardly bear to leave, the room with the blackboards, the room with the glass cabinet, the room with the most memories from four years of constant residency. 218 was more than a room, it was a place to grow.

TEACHING IS HARD WORK, AND NO one understands that better than teachers themselves. That's why the National Education Association celebrates National Teacher Appreciation Week every year in May. The NEA encourages communities nationwide to honor their local educators and let them know their dedication is appreciated.

TIP: *Looking for an end-of-year teacher gift? Just cover a box with school-themed papers of your choosing (there are many available!), create a note about what might go inside, and give it to your favorite teacher with an apple and a thank you card.*

Why I Became a Teacher

I became a teacher because I love people, and specifically because I love high-school aged kids. I became a teacher because I wanted to repay my own wonderful teachers: Mrs. Rohlf, Mr. Putka, Mr. Kibler. I became a teacher because I was angry at the bad teachers I had (who shall remain unnamed). I became a teacher because I am passionate about details of the world. I became a teacher because history is a story, full of excitement and intrigue and interest. I became a teacher because I love summer. I became a teacher because it is in my blood. I became a teacher because I wanted to serve.

Learned From Students

- Kids are not stupid.

- The most important thing a teacher can do is take a real interest in his or her students. The rest will fall in place.

- Stories are better than lectures, even if they are the same thing.

- Teachers aren't friends. They might be like big sisters on occasion, but not friends.

- Whatever I'm teaching is the least important thing some days. There's a heck of a lot more going on elsewhere.

- Busywork is not cool. Real work is better.

- Food days buy two months of good behavior.

- So does picking the NCAA Final Four and champion with 100% accuracy.

Delphian

The vocal music program was one of the highlights of Great Falls High. I was lucky to be asked to travel with Delphian Choir on tour while I taught, and even luckier to be asked to accompany from time to time. And the destinations... what a wonderful opportunity to visit places I'd never been: Calgary, Vancouver, Seattle, Tacoma, Spokane, Sheridan, Casper, Colorado Springs, Moscow, ID... I loved traveling with these kids. I loved spending the extra time with Robin. I loved listening to them sing. I've never heard anything like it before or since: so much talent and dedication!

The Wrath of Dillow

I have a long line. I learned early on that it's best to pick your battles with high school kids. Don't pick at things that aren't such a big deal, because you'll drive yourself crazy. Be sure to laugh with them. Treat them with respect and let them talk, never forgetting to listen. Let them be a little goofy sometimes. A classroom where students and teacher aren't afraid to laugh together is healthy.

But.

If you cross my long line, be warned: I will turn into a raging, livid lunatic. I won't yell, but I might make you cry. Not on purpose... just by the sheer scariness I will exude. I can count on my left hand the number of times it happened. But it was enough to let them know that they better watch it.

I was inspired by National Teacher Appreciation Week to create a tribute to my own teaching career. I wanted a place to collect and display a few of the little mementos and memories I gathered while I was teaching. Another motivation is my wish that I knew more about my relatives. I come from a long line of teachers and would love to know more about their experiences in the classroom. I sat down over the course of a few evenings and typed out memories, details, and facts about my time in the classroom to print on little tags that fit inside the box. Hopefully there will be a curious teacher or two in the generations that follow me.

May 1

Mother Goose Day

4¾ x 7 accordion album

This photo was taken at Mother Goose Land (despite the fact that I'm standing next to Wizard of Oz characters) in Canton, Ohio, probably in 1977 or 1978. Mother Goose Land only exists in memory now—it is officially categorized as a defunct amusement park—but when I was little, it was larger than life and only a short drive from Grandma Watson's house in Massillon.

THE MOTHER GOOSE SOCIETY WAS founded in 1987 by Gloria T. Delamar, author of *Mother Goose: From Nursery to Literature,* to increase awareness of the great historical importance of old nursery rhymes. For hundreds of years, the simple verses have been shared and passed from generation to generation to teach morals, provide comfort, and connect with the past. Artist Mary Englebreit said it best: "Mother Goose rhymes meet children at eye level with their colorful characters, disarming honesty, and playful feeling for life."

I collect Mother Goose books as a way to honor my Grandma Watson and thank my mama for the countless hours they both spent reading to me—Mother Goose rhymes and any other book I requested. By compiling this small accordion book, I can introduce my daughters to the great-grandmother they never met and let them know what they share with her: a head full of rhyme and imagination. For me, finding connections like these is what scrapbooking is all about.

DATE

First Saturday in May

EVENT

National

Scrapbooking Day

WHY DO YOU SCRAPBOOK? A SCRAPBOOKING "mission statement" isn't a new concept by any means, but if you've never created one, make it a priority this month! If you're new to scrapbooking, jot down a few lines about what you hope to gain from the hobby. If you've been at it for years and are starting to recognize its impact in your life, capture those thoughts on paper.

I scrapbook because I love to take photos.

I scrapbook because I love words.

I scrapbook because I love to tell stories.

I scrapbook because I forget things too easily if I keep them only in my head. I scrapbook because I wonder what it was like for my ancestors to raise children, keep a home, and live a fulfilling life and I don't want anyone to wonder what it was like for me someday. I scrapbook because I don't want to forget what raising children, keeping a home, and living a fulfilling life was like. I scrapbook because I want my children to know how funny they were when they were little. I scrapbook because I want my children to know how much they are loved as they grow bigger. I scrapbook because I love pretty paper and good design. I scrapbook because it's the art I've been searching for my entire life.

Time flies, so I scrapbook.
ED

12 x 12 page

TIP: *I found this beautiful card in Manhattan Beach, California, and knew I had to have it—not to send, of course, but to use as scrapbooking inspiration. Keep your eyes open for items that inspire you. Then repeat after me: I don't have to reinvent the wheel every time I scrapbook. Next time you find yourself staring blankly at a bare sheet of cardstock, repeat that mantra. Really.*

NO DATE IN THE 1940S WAS MORE WELCOMED than May 8, the day the Allies of World War II accepted the unconditional surrender of Nazi Germany. Enormous celebrations ensued throughout the United States and Europe, especially in England where years of war had taken a terrible toll on the civilian population. Even future queen Princess Elizabeth and her sister Princess Margaret were permitted to join in the celebrations in London, anonymously wandering through the crowds.

Rememberance is universal.

Veterans Day in the United States, Rememberance Sunday or "Poppy Day" in November in the UK, and Bastille Day in France are just a few of the occasions to remember and thank those who have ensured our safety and freedom.

Rememberance spans continents, even generations and unites us as thankful and compassionate human beings.

We remember those who went before us, those who were lost, and those who came back.

But mostly we remember the sacrifices of the the men and women, who believed in something so great, that they were willing to die for it, if they had to.

I am proud to know these people and call them my family.

He that cannot endure the Bad will not live to see the Good.
— JEWISH PROVERB

Inspired by the military service rendered by several of her relatives, Anna created this 4 x 4 mini-album chock-full of extraordinary family photos. She started with World War II, when both her grandfathers served in the British Army, her grandmother worked as a seamstress to support the war effort, and her great-aunt worked for the fire department at home. But once she realized how much of her family's history is intertwined with the military, she expanded her focus to stretch back to her great-great-uncle Willy's service in World War I and forward to her sister's service in the Iraq War. Just because your project starts out looking one way doesn't mean it has to end up that same way. Don't be afraid to change your focus: sometimes the most meaningful albums are created because of this flexibility. No rules = more freedom to create!

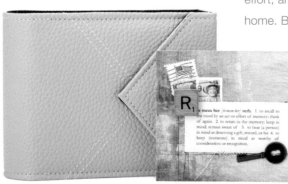

4 x 4 mini-album
by Anna Aspnes

Great Great Uncle Harry was injured by shrapnel and had to have 4 inches removed from his leg, which was replaced by a steel peg and a raised shoe. He had left his sweetheart behind to fight for his country, but when he returned home, he refused to marry her because he did not want her to be burdened by a cripple.

Grandma Day did not serve in a military sense. She worked beside her sister, Kitty, as a Seamstress in a factory called Tap and Toothills, and supported her country by sewing parachutes and decoys.

Sarah did a 6 month deployment in Basra, Iraq in 2004-2005. She lived in a ruin of a hotel, told us of children being shot or maimed by unexploded amunition by playing in their streets, and told us of the plot by Guerilla groups to kidnap Captain Sarah and hold for her for ransom.

હોસ્કર; વરૂણ મોટરના સ્ટોકીસ્ટ
ગ્રી'ઝ, બૉલ બેરી'ગ, ઓસ, બેલ્ટ
તથા

THE CHILDREN'S BOOK COUNCIL SPONSORS Children's Book Week each year to encourage children to "discover the complexity of the world beyond their own experience through books."

I love children's books. Not only because they provide welcome variety in my days at home with my daughters, but also because they are a never-ending source of inspiration for scrapbook pages. The page I made for Gracie on her 14-month "birthday" was inspired by one of my favorite children's illustrators, Melissa Sweet. So as you celebrate Children's Book Week at your local library or bookstore this year, be sure to do some design browsing, too.

12 x 12 page

DATE

Late May

EVENT

National Geography Bee

Who would have guessed that a simple little song could develop in you a love of geography as well? But that's what happens when you listen to **They Might Be Giants**, possibly one of our favorite children's bands. The funny thing is that I used to listen to them

aLgeria

To ZiMBaBWe

way back when (way back!) before I was even married and most definitely before I had any kids. Thankfully, they've since ventured into the kids market (smart guys!) and we have supported them ever since. Alphabet of Nations, on the "Here Come the ABCs" album is the song I'm referring to by the way. In the song, they list a country for every letter of the alphabet...well, I guess West Xylophone doesn't technically count, right? Combine the song with a ten dollar globe from Target and we have ourselves a geography expert. You can now locate all the countries that they sing about on your globe...and then some. Don't you love it when learning is this fun and easy?   C3/07

8½ x 11 page

by Margaret Scarbrough

TIP: *Margaret created her circle frame with an X-Acto knife and a piece of patterned paper. After carefully cutting out the inside, she manually formatted the text in Microsoft Word with tabs and spaces so it would fit neatly within the border.*

EACH MAY THE NATIONAL Geographic Society sponsors the National Geographic Bee, a competition in which thousands of American students from grades four through eight compete to answer really, really hard geography questions. (Think I'm kidding? Do you know which European river the Port of Rotterdam is built on?)

Margaret loves the music of They Might Be Giants: it's hip, funny, and never boring. Imagine her surprise when she discovered how educational it was, too! After a few listens to "Alphabet of Nations," her son Matthew's interest in those countries blossomed into a full-fledged desire to learn where in the world all those places were. As parents, it's sometimes hard to pinpoint just when a love of learning starts—things happen so fast—so Margaret made sure to document this story before it was forgotten.

NOTE: *I might be biased because of my background as a history teacher, but I'm willing to claim that a basic understanding of geography can make you a better scrapbooker. Asking yourself questions about the places in your life can help you see yourself and your surroundings in a new way.*

1
2
3
4
5
6
7
8
9
10
11
12
13
14
15
16
17
18
19
20
21
22
23
24
25
26
27
28
29
30

This month...

go take a hike

send a letter far away

honor someone's fight against cancer

pay tribute to America's national pastime

savor the simple things and scream with glee

spend a day surrounded by nature

remember a road trip

hike

OUR JOURNEY TO THE TOP OF MT. WASHBURN

WHETHER YOU'RE AFTER A RELAXING STROLL or a strenuous workout, National Trails Day is a perfect opportunity to grab your hiking partner and your camera and head into the great outdoors for some fresh air and a fresh perspective. And while you're out there, remember to be grateful for the thousands of volunteers who work tirelessly to maintain our nation's recreational trails.

driving south

ALONG THE WINDING HIGHWAY INTO YELLOWSTONE NATIONAL PARK, WE WATCHED THE SUN PLAY HIDE-N-SEEK IN THE CLOUDS. AS THE SKY WASHED TO A DIRTY GREY, I LOOKED OUT THE CAR WINDOW AT THE SCATTERED BISON, STANDING SHAGGY AND DAMP, IN THE SUMMER RAIN. I WONDERED TO MYSELF IF WE WOULD STILL GO ON OUR HIKE. BUT I SHOULD HAVE KNOWN BETTER. I SHOULD HAVE KNOWN THAT MY FAMILY WOULD NOT BE DETERRED BY A LITTLE SPATTER OF RAIN, OR SLEET, OR SNOW. HIKING MT. WASHBURN IS A TRADITION OF SORTS, A TRADITION THAT DOES NOT ALLOW FOR INDECISION BASED ON FICKLE WEATHER CONDITIONS. EVEN IF YOU ONLY PACKED CAPRI PANTS AND RUNNERS. AND SO AS WE STEPPED OUT OF THE CAR AND SAW THE FOG CURLING AROUND THE TREES, WE SIMPLY CINCHED OUR PACKS A LITTLE TIGHTER AND BEGAN TO HIKE.

6 x 6 mini-album
by Mary MacAskill

It's not every day you get to see the top of the world. Thinking about the significance of National Trails Day, Mary was inspired to create a remarkable album about her hiking adventure to the top of Mt. Washburn in Yellowstone National Park. She kept her design simple, pairing photos from the climb with actual maps. For a unique touch, she cut a hole in each page to allow the compass on the back page to peek through the entire album.

NOTE: *The American Hiking Society sponsors a National Trails Day Photo Contest in conjunction with National Trails Day. Hint, hint. Visit americanhiking.org to enter.*

the trail

WAS SLICK AND SCATTERED WITH MUDDY PUDDLES OF WATER. AS THE TRAIL TWISTED UP THE MOUNTAIN, THE DRIPPING TREES WERE LEFT BEHIND, AND WITH HOODS PULLED UP, WE FACED AN OPEN WIND. AS WE CLIMBED HIGHER THE RAIN TURNED TO SLEET AND THEN TO SNOW. IT WAS JUNE 15, MOM'S 54TH BIRTHDAY, AND FOR HER BIRTHDAY, SHE WANTED TO HIKE MT. WASHBURN, SO THERE WAS NO TURNING AROUND, SNOW OR NOT.

I HIKED WITH MOM — OR AT LEAST ATTEMPTED TO KEEP UP WITH HER PACE — AND WE CHATTED OUR WAY ACROSS THE SNOW PACKED TRAILS. I DON'T REMEMBER EVERYTHING WE TALKED ABOUT AND, EVEN THOUGH I WAS SHIVERING AND MY RUNNERS WERE SQUISHING WITH WATER, I REALLY ENJOYED THE CHANCE TO SPEND TIME WITH HER. ESPECIALLY ON HER BIRTHDAY.

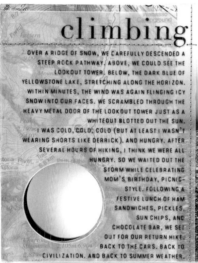

climbing

OVER A RIDGE OF SNOW, WE CAREFULLY DESCENDED A STEEP ROCK PATHWAY. ABOVE, WE COULD SEE THE LOOKOUT TOWER. BELOW, THE DARK BLUE OF YELLOWSTONE LAKE, STRETCHING ALONG THE HORIZON. WITHIN MINUTES, THE WIND WAS AGAIN FLINGING ICY SNOW INTO OUR FACES. WE SCRAMBLED THROUGH THE HEAVY METAL DOOR OF THE LOOKOUT TOWER JUST AS A WHITEOUT BLOTTED OUT THE SUN. I WAS COLD, COLD, COLD (BUT AT LEAST I WASN'T WEARING SHORTS LIKE DERRICK). AND HUNGRY. AFTER SEVERAL HOURS OF HIKING, I THINK WE WERE ALL HUNGRY. SO WE WAITED OUT THE STORM WHILE CELEBRATING MOM'S BIRTHDAY, PICNIC-STYLE. FOLLOWING A FESTIVE LUNCH OF HAM SANDWICHES, PICKLES, SUN CHIPS, AND CHOCOLATE BAR, WE SET OUT FOR OUR RETURN HIKE. BACK TO THE CARS. BACK TO CIVILIZATION. AND BACK TO SUMMER WEATHER.

OUR LAST VIEW FROM THE TOP OF MT. WASHBURN, AS WE TURNED TO GO HOME.

the end

[END] — NOUN. THE FURTHERMOST IMAGINABLE PLACE OR POINT; TERMINATION OR CONCLUSION; THE CONCLUDING PART

DATE

June 1

EVENT

Pen Pal Day

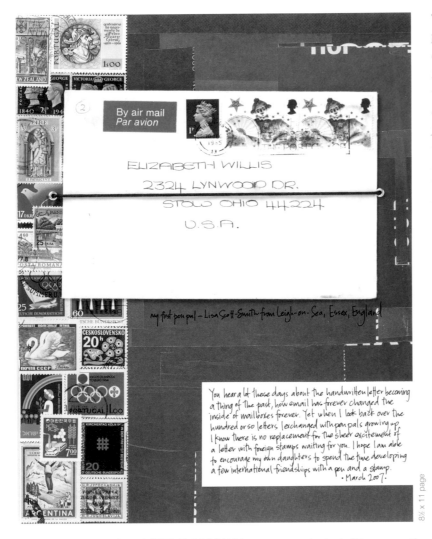

ELIZABETH WILLIS
2324 LYNWOOD DR.
STOLO OHIO 44224
U.S.A.

my first pen pal – Lisa Scott-Smith from Leigh-on-Sea, Essex, England

You hear a lot these days about the handwritten letter becoming a thing of the past, how email has forever changed the inside of mailboxes forever. Yet when I look back over the hundred or so letters I exchanged with pen pals growing up, I know there is no replacement for the sheer excitement of a letter with foreign stamps waiting for you. I hope I am able to encourage my own daughters to spend the time developing a few international friendships with a pen and a stamp.
                                        - March 2007.

8½ x 11 page

TIP: *I wanted my first pen pal letter to be accessible on this page, so I created an elastic band to hold it to the page. You can do the same thing. Just thread elastic through two set eyelets and knot it off in the back, adjusting the tension before tying the second knot.*

PEN PAL DAY IS A LITTLE-KNOWN observance that celebrates the relationships created through long-distance correspondence.

I love mail. Always have, always will. You can imagine my excitement when I discovered the world of pen pals as an elementary school student: "You mean there are wordy little girls all over the world who love mail as much as I do?" I still get excited by letters stamped with foreign postmarks appearing in my mailbox. This passion for mail and international culture is definitely a part of my life story that deserves to be documented.

First Sunday in June

National Cancer

Survivors Day

12 x 12 page
by Mi'Chelle Larsen

LET
NOTHING
STAND
IN
YOUR
WAY

NOT EVEN CANCER

an important lesson I'm
learning from Dave, who pushes
himself to the limits following his
passions in a situation where
many others would have
resigned to the mundane.

THERE ARE NEARLY 11 MILLION CANCER survivors in the United States alone, many of whom are still courageously battling the disease. (The National Cancer Survivors Day Foundation defines a survivor as anyone now living who has ever been diagnosed with cancer.) On National Cancer Survivors Day, events are held in hundreds of communities nationwide to offer hope and support to those whose lives have been affected by cancer, including the survivors themselves as well as their family and friends.

Mi'Chelle created this powerful page about her uncle's fight against a cancerous brain tumor. The layout not only honors his spirit but also reminds her to maintain hers. After five surgeries, he must work hard in physical therapy to regain his skills; Mi'Chelle is inspired by his resilience in the face of such difficulties. Do you know someone living with a devastating cancer diagnosis? Make a layout that shows just how much you care.

June 12, 1939

Dedication of Baseball

Hall of Fame

THE BASEBALL HALL OF FAME IS LOCATED IN a little village in central New York State called Cooperstown, where baseball is said to have originated. Hundreds of thousands of people travel to the hall each year to pay tribute to the game's greatest players.

8½ x 11 page
by Laura Kurz

Laura's layout about her husband's trip to Cooperstown shares his excitement at having seen so many traces and artifacts of the baseball history they both grew up hearing about from their fathers. These little bits of family lore and experience are the threads that weave through generations, and capturing them on a scrapbook page will provide a starting point for a new generation to "talk baseball" one day.

June 13, 1884

Introduction of First

Roller Coaster in

the U.S.

DID YOU KNOW THAT THE CONCEPT OF ROLLER coasters originated in Russia in the form of speedy ice slides built in the 1600s? Since that time, roller coasters have steadily developed into the thrill rides we know (and love) today, having gained a corkscrew here or a loop there along the way.

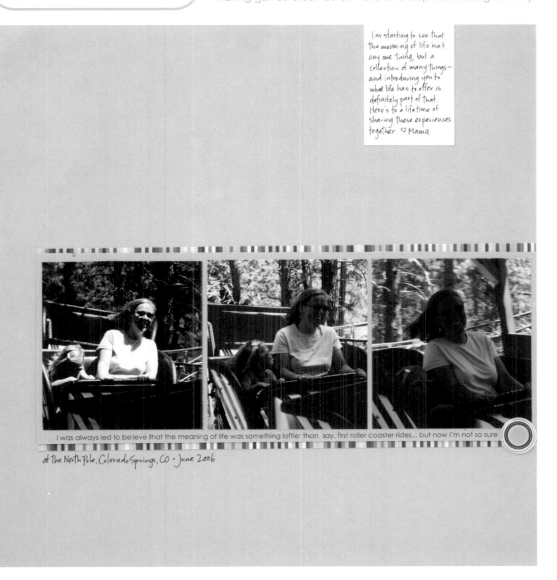

I'm starting to see that the meaning of life isn't any one thing, but a collection of many things—and introducing you to what life has to offer is definitely part of that. Here's to a lifetime of sharing these experiences together ♡ Mama

I was always led to believe that the meaning of life was something loftier than, say, first roller coaster rides... but now I'm not so sure

at the North Pole, Colorado Springs, CO · June 2006

12 x 12 page

TIP: *Do you have only blurry or dark photos from an especially meaningful event? Use them anyway. The fond memories you have from the experience will easily overshadow the quality of your photographs. Life is not about perfection!*

I don't remember my first ride on a roller coaster, but I'll never forget Maddie's first experience with speed and metal and whirly turns—specially designed to make a four-year-old scream with glee. I wanted to remember how good it feels to introduce my daughter to something new, surely one of the great joys of parenthood. For that reason, this page is just as much about me as it is about her.

WHILE YOU'RE OUT AND ABOUT THIS MONTH exploring the trails in your area, be sure to look around you. It's a great time of year to capture the beauty of nature, especially since Nature Photography Day, sponsored by the North American Nature Photography Association, falls smack in the middle of June.

[split second]

where adventure, patience, anticipation, folly, and luck intersected

Vedawoo, Wyoming • Summer 2000

11 x 8½ page

Before our girls were born, Matt and I would take off for long days wandering around the wilderness of Montana and Wyoming, my camera and a few water bottles our only luggage. (We haven't traveled so light since!) I wanted this photo, taken on my old film Canon Rebel, to be the focus of my super-simple layout. Believe it or not, I finished the layout in less time than it took me to capture this lucky image. Matt and I don't have the time to roam the countryside as much as we once did, but this page reminds me how much I love spending time outdoors, just waiting for the split second when I can see something amazing.

June 29, 1956

Introduction of Interstate Highway System

12 x 12 page

BEFORE PRESIDENT EISENHOWER signed the Federal-Aid Highway Act of 1956, the United States was a wildly different place than it is now. Today more than 46,000 miles of highway connect towns and cities in every direction, but before those roads were built, cross-country travel was significantly slower and more scenic than it is today.

In honor of our country's vast roadways, June is a perfect time to tell your best road trip stories.

Whether a road trip is successful or disastrous, it always makes for an interesting anecdote. And there are so many cool travel products on the market that putting together a coordinated page is a snap!

TIP: It may seem obvious, but it took me years to discover this little trick: while adhering my journaling transparency to my page, I hid the adhesive behind my photo and the "WY" stickers. It's like magic!

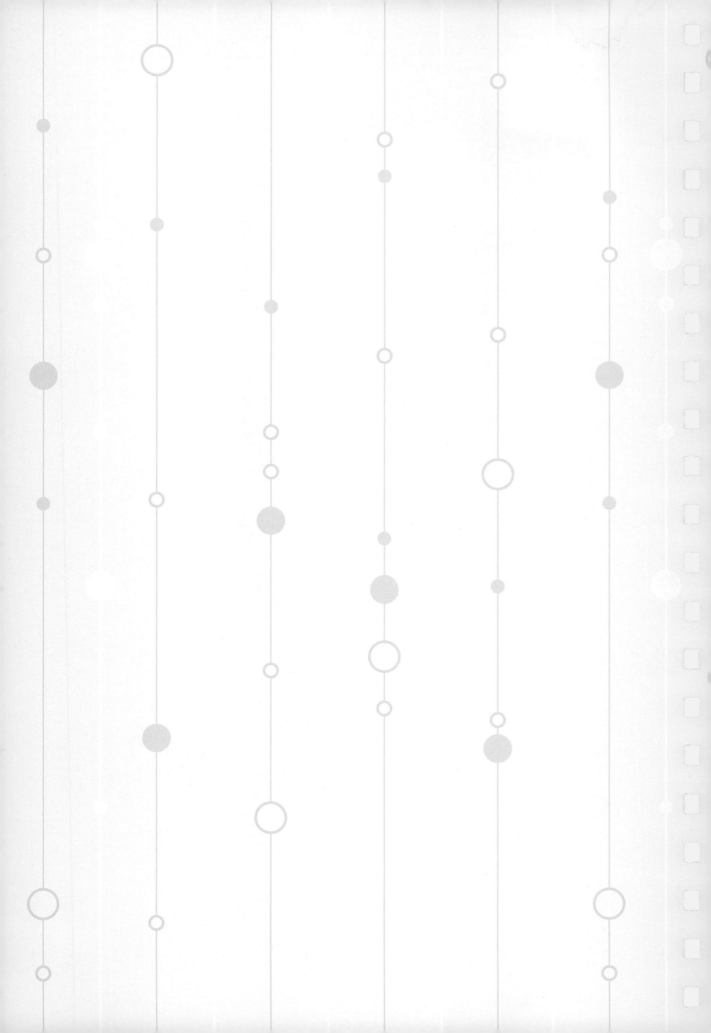

1
2
3
4
5
6
7
8
9
10
11
12
13
14
15
16
17
18
19
20
21
22
23
24
25
26
27
28
29
30
31

This month...

consider the significance of the zoo

explore the design possibilities of the humble postage stamp

let five little numbers tell a story

commemorate your country of birth

uncover the mysteries of your (tender) heart

bring some folk wisdom to your pages

tell the real (not-so-dreamy) story

say thank you for acts of love, big and small

soak up colorful inspiration everywhere

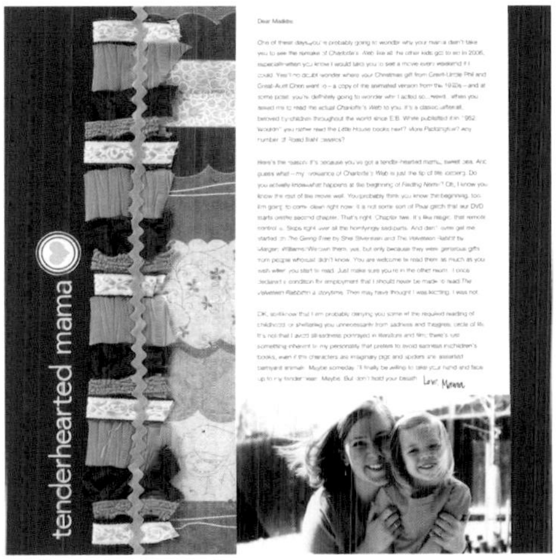

tenderhearted mama

THE PHILADELPHIA ZOO OPENED IN 1874 with 813 animals and a vision: to conserve, to educate, and to further a sense of stewardship of the natural world. Admission cost 25 cents for adults and 10 cents for children. Admission prices to zoos throughout the country have gone up just a bit since the 1800s, but the mission remains the same: to encourage scientific study and stewardship of the natural world.

Colorado Springs, CO • Cleveland, OH • Oakland, CA

let's go.

12 x 12 spread

I haven't always loved zoos. I have memories of visiting them growing up, and while I'm sure I had fun at the time, they didn't leave an indelible mark upon my heart as a place I truly loved to go. Reading accounts of poorly maintained zoos soured me on the existence of zoos in general, believing them to be no more than sad circus sideshows exploiting wild animals for profit. Wouldn't animals be better off in their natural habitats? I wrote them off entirely, not stepping foot into another zoo throughout college and for years after. Having children changes everything, they say. I had no idea this cliché would extend to my feelings about zoos, too.

After we moved to Colorado Springs in 2003 we decided to get a zoo membership, mostly to have a reasonably interesting place to occasionally take Maddie. We'd heard relatively good things about the giraffe exhibit there from friends who also had memberships. I think we were hooked from the first visit. Our visions of occasional visits turned into a reality of frequent visits, never tiring of seeing the same animals on a different day. Cheyenne Mountain Zoo became a magical place first for Maddie, then for Gracie.

Zoos are different places entirely with small children in tow. A well-maintained, modern zoo becomes an absolute treasure trove of learning experiences; animals that exist only in books suddenly appear in full color—close enough to really observe, even for a baby. Over the course of the last four years we've seen an amazing amount of learning occur for both Maddie and Gracie as they discover the diversity of the natural world, eager to see and learn more. We belong to the Oakland Zoo now; another move will bring another zoo. I am a convert: there is no better way to introduce real science to children than this.

Here's a great approach for scrapbooking a recurring event. Instead of plopping your photos on a page and describing who, what, and when (year after year after year), narrow down your photos (or just choose one favorite) and journal about why you visit this place and how you feel about it. I've got plenty of wild animal photos to go around from scores of zoo visits. Using some of those photos to illustrate my feelings about taking my children to the zoo has injected a breath of fresh air into a worn-out topic. You don't need to dig this deep with every set of photos you scrapbook, but a little soul-searching here and there can add variety to your albums.

July 1, 1847

First U.S. Postage

Stamps Issued

8½ x 11 page
by Laura Kurz

POSTAGE STAMPS WERE created in Great Britain in 1840. Seven years later, the United States issued its own postage stamps with Benjamin Franklin (5 cents) and George Washington (10 cents) depicted. Since that time, thousands of subjects have graced the tiny canvases, from teddy bears to Elvis, to outer space, to coral reefs.

Securing a spot on a U.S. postage stamp has always been a difficult endeavor—proposals must be submitted 3 years in advance for consideration. But Stamps.com has just made it easier. Their PhotoStamps program allows customers to upload their own images to create legal postage stamps approved by the U.S. Postal Service. Laura uploaded one of her father's original art pieces and turned it into a postage stamp suitable for mailing (and scrapbooking). Her minimalist design allows the tiny stamp to shine on her page.

IN 1963 THE U.S. POSTAL SERVICE introduced the "zip code" system, designed to manage the increase in the volume of mail and to ensure more reliable mail delivery. Since that time, zip codes have taken on geographic significance as well. (Just think of all the drama the zip code 90210 held for TV lovers everywhere in the 1990s.)

My life is neatly divided into zip codes: the one where I was born and raised (44224), the one where I attended college (45056), and then a quick succession of new zip codes after I married into the U.S. Air Force and found myself moving every few years. For me, zip codes aren't just little numbers that make a job easier for the post office; they're the titles of chapters in my life story. It occurred to me that this would be a perfect way to create a little album about the places I've lived since 1995. After a lifetime of moving around so much, I know I'll appreciate having this reminder of where we lived and when!

VARIATION: *You might not move around as much as I do, but you can still create your own zip code album based on where dear friends and family live, places you'd like to visit, or past vacation destinations. All it takes is a photo, a handful of memories, a label or tag with the zip code—and you're done!*

We are an Air Force family.

★

This means a lot of things.

As far as our living arrangements go, it means we don't live in the same place for very long. It means that after a while, we start to mix up our addresses and phone numbers when asked to provide them. It means we have the opportunity to live in many types of places, in many different neighborhoods, with all sorts of people. It means that every so often we have to leave a place we've grown to love, and that's difficult to do. It means we have to carry our home within us, because the places we call home aren't permanent.

We have to make them ours while we can.

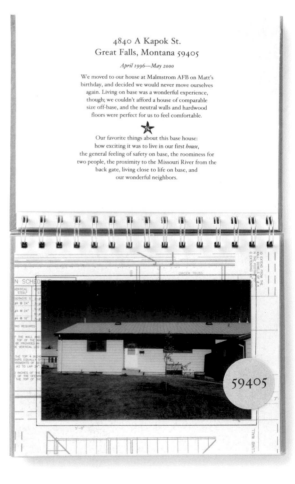

4840 A Kapok St.
Great Falls, Montana 59405

April 1996—May 2000

We moved to our house at Malmstrom AFB on Matt's birthday, and decided we would never move ourselves again. Living on base was a wonderful experience, though; we couldn't afford a house of comparable size off-base, and the neutral walls and hardwood floors were perfect for us to feel comfortable.

★

Our favorite things about this base house: how exciting it was to live in our first *house*, the general feeling of safety on base, the roominess for two people, the proximity to the Missouri River from the back gate, living close to life on base, and our wonderful neighbors.

59405

5 × 7 mini-album

Tip: My Grandma Rinehart always taught me to finish the backs of my craft projects (whether it's needlepoint or framed art). Here's a peek at the back of my "By Zip" album. To see the backs of other projects from this book, visit simplescrapbooksmag.com/almanac.

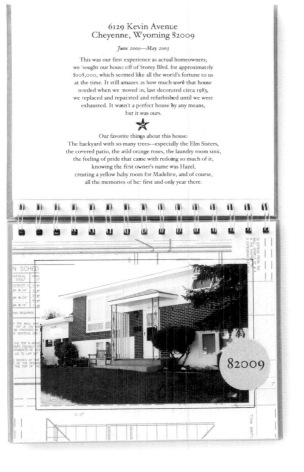

6129 Kevin Avenue
Cheyenne, Wyoming 82009

June 2006—May 2003

This was our first experience as actual homeowners; we bought our house off of Storey Blvd. for approximately $108,000, which seemed like all the world's fortune to us at the time. It still amazes as how much *work* that house needed when we moved in; last decorated circa 1983, we replaced and repainted and refurbished until we were exhausted. It wasn't a perfect house by any means, but it was ours.

Our favorite things about this house:
The backyard with so many trees—especially the Elm Sisters, the covered patio, the wild orange roses, the laundry room sink, the feeling of pride that came with redoing so much of it, knowing the first owner's name was Hazel, creating a yellow baby room for Madeline, and of course, all the memories of her first and only year there.

6185 Hearth Court
Colorado Springs, Colorado 80922

June 2003—June 2006

Our house on Hearth Ct. was our second experience as homeowners, and we definitely learned some lessons this time around (namely, to buy a house that didn't need so much work). We purchased it for $191,500 which made our first house seem like a paltry little purchase. We made some changes to make it ours, and were very comfortable for the three years we lived here.

Our favorite things about this house:
The backyard, the trail that was just outside our fence, the garden, the two trees we planted (hawthorn in back, apple in front), the cul-de-sac for riding bikes with our good, friendly neighbors, my craft room in the basement, creating a green garden room for Gracie, and all the memories we made with our girls there.

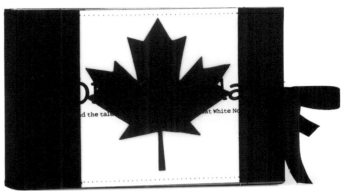

4 x 6 mini-album
by Mary MacAskill

Tip: *Mary added a clever touch to the back of her "Oh, Canada!" album. Visit simplescrapbooksmag.com/almanac to see the backs of other projects in this book!*

EACH YEAR ON JULY 1 OUR NEIGHBORS TO THE north celebrate Canada Day, which marks the formation of the Dominion of Canada, comprised of four original provinces— Nova Scotia, New Brunswick, Ontario, and Quebec. Today, Canada is a federation made up of ten provinces and three territories.

Mary is an American who married Derrick, a Canadian. She knew that one day their daughter, Sadie Jane, would be curious about her family's geographic origins. So in honor of Canada Day, she created this little album to share their story and teach a few Canadian facts along the way. Her trademark machine stitching provides an elegant design element that recalls a flag.

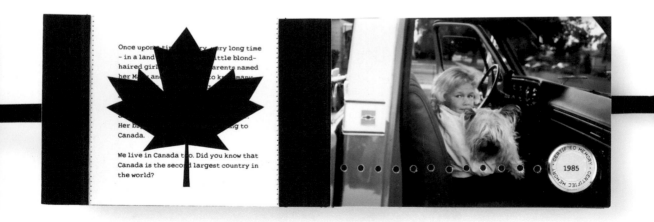

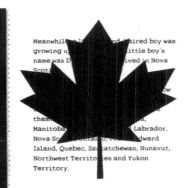

Meanwhile a little blond-haired boy was growing up too. That little boy's name was D... ... lived in Nova Scoti...

them... ...ow
Manitoba... ...Labrador,
Nova Sc... ...ontario, ...dward
Island, Quebec, Saskatchewan, Nunavut,
Northwest Territories and Yukon
Territory.

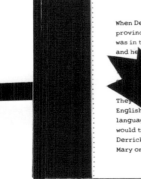
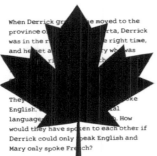

When Derrick gr... ...e moved to the
province of... ...rta, Derrick
was in the r... ...e right time,
and he met a... ...ry who was
...r... ...ch...

They... ...oke
English... ...al
language... ...h. How
would they have spoken to each other if
Derrick could only speak English and
Mary only spoke French?

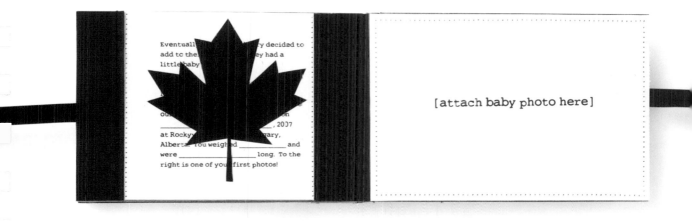

Eventually... ...ry decided to
add to the... ...ey had a
little baby...

... ...
ou... ...n
_____, 2007
at Rocky... ...gary,
Albert... You weighed _____ and
were _____ long. To the
right is one of your first photos!

[attach baby photo here]

July 11

E.B. White's Birthday

E. B. WHITE IS MOST FAMOUS FOR HIS timeless children's books, but he's also known for modernizing the classic writing handbook, *The Elements of Style*. Advocating simplicity in writing, White wanted to "make every word tell"—a lesson scrapbookers can take to heart!

tenderhearted mama

Dear Maddie,

One of these days you're probably going to wonder why your mama didn't take you to see the remake of *Charlotte's Web* like all the other kids got to do in 2006, especially when you know I would take you to see a movie every weekend if I could. You'll no doubt wonder where your Christmas gift from Great-Uncle Phil and Great-Aunt Cheri went to—a copy of the animated version from the 1970s—and at some point, you're definitely going to wonder why I acted so...weird...when you asked me to read the actual *Charlotte's Web* to you. It's a classic, after all, beloved by children throughout the world since E.B. White published it in 1952. Wouldn't you rather read the *Little House* books next? More *Paddington*? Any number of Roald Dahl classics?

Here's the reason: it's because you've got a tender-hearted mama, sweet pea. And guess what—my avoidance of *Charlotte's Web* is just the tip of the iceberg. Do you actually *know* what happens at the beginning of *Finding Nemo*? Oh, I know you know the rest of the movie well. You probably think you know the beginning, too. I'm going to come clean right now: it is not some sort of Pixar glitch that our DVD starts on the second chapter. That's right. Chapter two. It's like magic, that remote control is. Skips right over all the horrifyingly sad parts. And don't even get me started on *The Giving Tree* by Shel Silverstein and *The Velveteen Rabbit* by Margery Williams. We own them, yes, but only because they were generous gifts from people who just didn't know. You are welcome to read them as much as you wish when you start to read. Just make sure you're in the other room. I once declared a condition for employment that I should never be made to read *The Velveteen Rabbit* in a storytime. They may have thought I was kidding. I was not.

OK, so I know that I am probably denying you some of the required reading of childhood, or sheltering you unnecessarily from sadness and the great circle of life. It's not that I avoid all sadness portrayed in literature and film; there's just something inherent to my personality that prefers to avoid sadness in children's books, even if the characters are imaginary pigs and spiders and assorted barnyard animals. Maybe someday I'll finally be willing to take your hand and face up to my tender heart. Maybe. But don't hold your breath. Love, Mama

12 x 12 page

Tip: *To overcome journaler's block, pretend you're writing a letter! I've found that my thoughts come easier when I'm writing a letter than when I'm trying to compose "journaling."*

E. B. White's classic *Charlotte's Web* consistently ranks in the top ten of all-time favorite children's books, but I'd rather read just about anything else. With all apologies to Mr. White on his birthday, I decided to explain my reasons in a letter to Maddie. I'm predicting she'll turn out just like me when it comes to heart-rending children's literature, and she'll want to know why.

July 14

Woody Guthrie's

Birthday

WOODY GUTHRIE, ONE OF THE MOST PROLIFIC songwriters and folk musicians of the 20th century, was born in 1912 in Okemah, Oklahoma. He lived through tragedy and loss, but always managed to find solace and hope in the lyrics—almost 3,000 songs worth—he wrote as he traveled throughout the United States, lending his voice to the poor Americans he met along the way. While he is primarily known for his persistent social activism, Guthrie loved children (he had eight) and writing children's music.

Howdy little newlycome

I'll sing to you my song
I'd like to tell you all about the place you just came from…
I'll tell you how you found your way to the world here where you're born…
You'll tell me how you found your way to the world here where you're born.

— Woody Guthrie

5 days old

Bridget Sophia

12 x 12 page

I chose a small section of a track Guthrie recorded in his kitchen in 1951 to serve as a welcome for our own little newlycome, Bridget, when she was just five days old. A few buttons, a little string, and a photo—it doesn't get much simpler for a new mama than that.

99

WHEN WALT DISNEY HIRED THE STANFORD Research Institute to help him realize his vision of a magical park filled with wild animals, mountains, castles, rockets, princesses, and a big mouse, no one could have imagined that the 160-acre plot of land in Anaheim, California, would one day be one of the most storied destinations of all time. Disneyland opened after only a year of construction in July 1955, followed 16 years later by Walt Disney World in Orlando, Florida.

12 x 12 spread
by Anna Aspnes

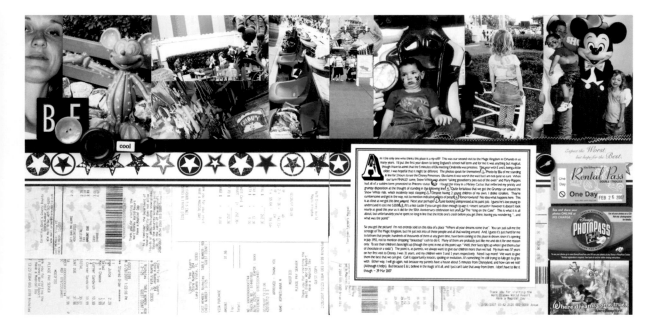

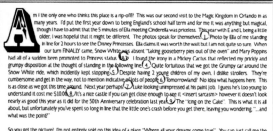

If you've been to either Disneyland or Walt Disney World, you no doubt have plenty of stories and photos to remind you of the magic (or lack thereof). Anna's experience at Walt Disney World was less than magical, as she watched both her money and patience fly off into Neverland by the end of the first day. While you don't want to taint someone else's memories of their Disney adventure (read: rain on your kid's parade) it's absolutely OK to document the reality of a dream vacation—that the reality isn't always a dream! Anna's wry sense of humor paints a picture of their visit that is sure to entertain her children one day while giving her a chuckle right now.

Fourth Sunday in July

Parents' Day

for not making too big a fuss when I decided to forgo my free education at the University of Akron and go to Miami instead

for buying me lots of art supplies, especially my Faber-Castell colored pencils

for walking me down the aisle at my wedding

for reading 'Twas the Night Before Christmas every year

for trying to teach me to love golf as much as you do (sorry that didn't work out so well)

for taking me to work with you at Stow High School and the University of Akron

for taking me to Ohio State football games and skull sessions at St. John's Arena

for saving me the last sip of Dr. Pepper when it used to come in glass bottles

for encouraging my love of music

for driving me to piano lessons for so many years at the Troyers' house

for paying to store the green piano for me after we had Grandma's to use instead

for sending me lots of mail when I've lived far from home

for sending cards to commemorate special occasions in the lives of my high school and college friends

for playing close close far away

for taking me swimming at Maplewood practically every day of the summer while I was growing up

for sitting at ten years worth of softball games

for staying home to take care of me for 13 years

for buying books and taking me to the library so often

for making the one passenger at a time rule (even though I hated it)

for teaching me to drive a stick shift

for coming out to help after my girls were born

for encouraging my love of music

for always being so proud of me

12 x 12 page

IN 1994 A CONGRESSIONAL RESOLUTION was signed into law establishing the fourth Sunday of each July as Parents' Day, a day for "recognizing, uplifting, and supporting the role of parents in the rearing of children." It's a day to celebrate parenting as well as to acknowledge its crucial role in a successful society.

In honor of Parents' Day, I decided it would be a good time to thank my parents for just some of the hundreds of acts of love they've shown me in my life. While I've always appreciated their creativity, sacrifice and dedication in parenting me, writing this list made those gifts seem even more important.

July 28

Beatrix Potter's

Birthday

BEATRIX POTTER, A BRITISH AUTHOR, ARTIST, scientist, and conservationist born in 1866, is best known for her children's classic, *The Tale of Peter Rabbit*. Potter wrote a total of 23 books for children—all published in a format small enough for a child to hold and read. Her illustrations of ducks, kittens, squirrels, and rabbits are synonymous with the magic of childhood.

Inspired by a stack of Peter Rabbit postcards that had been sitting on her desk, Mi'Chelle created a sweet, tiny album that's just the right size for her son Owen's little hands. Originally thinking she would create a project with a more literal Peter Rabbit-inspired theme, she realized that she was most inspired by the soft color palette that is Potter's trademark. After deciding on a color scheme, Mi'Chelle's album came together seamlessly.

TIP: You've heard it before, but it bears repeating: inspiration is everywhere! Next time you're looking for an idea to incorporate in an album or page, stop and look through a "junk" drawer, bulletin board, or desk (as Mi'Chelle did) to find your next inspiration piece. Give yourself a chance to mull it over, too. Literal inspiration is terrific, but letting yourself be inspired by something more abstract is a fun way to push yourself creatively.

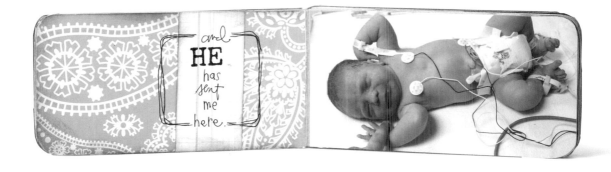

and **HE** has sent me here.

has **givEn** me an earthly home

With parents **kInd** and dear

my dear Owen,
It means a lot to this momma to remember that you were His child long before you were ever mine. I love you with all the power of my being and He loves you more than that. Don't forget it. ♡/ your mother

5¾ x 2¾ mini-album
by Mi'Chelle Larsen

1
2
3
4
5
6
7
8
9
10
11
12
13

14
15
16
17
18
19
20
21
22
23
24
25
26
27
28
29
30
31

no place like home

favorite place

KINDERGARTEN MARKS THE BEGINNING of a new era for children—a transition so big, it can also be a little scary! That's why author Katie Davis created Get Ready For Kindergarten Month, full of ideas and guidance for teachers, parents, and kids everywhere as they embark on this new adventure.

2006

2007

August 2006 — Age 5
You started kindergarten this month. Towards the end of summer, we began practicing writing your name, going over school etiquette, getting you back on schedule... basically, all the good stuff that would make the transition from preschool to kindergarten that much easier. And it paid off too! You had relatively few problems adjusting to a new classroom, new friends and a totally new school routine. Pretty good for my previously super shy boy.

January 2007 — Age 6
Somehow, we found ourselves moving cross-country to California this month (an unexpected move to be sure). Which, of course, meant that you had to start kindergarten all over again...and in the middle of the school year. Plus, school was now an hour longer and involved lunch as well. I thought for sure you would have a hard time of it all, but instead, you surprised us by jumping right in. Yup, you are a total kindergarten superstar!

kinDerGarten²

11 x 8½ page
by Margaret Scarbrough

Margaret's son Matthew started kindergarten twice (thanks to a cross-country move from Massachusetts to California in the middle of the school year), so she knows all too well the trepidation a five-year-old can feel getting ready for kindergarten! Even if your own children are long past kindergarten, chances are they still have memories of how they felt getting ready for the big day. Scrapbook them! There are some rites of passage in life that are too important to exclude from your albums.

DATE

August 1-31

EVENT

National Inventors' Month

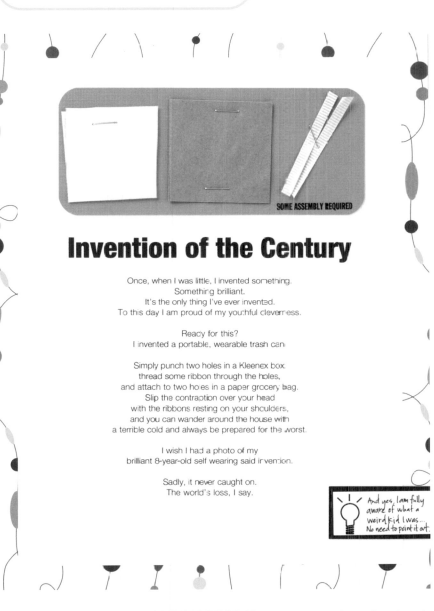

SOME ASSEMBLY REQUIRED

Invention of the Century

Once, when I was little, I invented something.
Something brilliant.
It's the only thing I've ever invented.
To this day I am proud of my youthful cleverness.

Ready for this?
I invented a portable, wearable trash can.

Simply punch two holes in a Kleenex box,
thread some ribbon through the holes,
and attach to two holes in a paper grocery bag.
Slip the contraption over your head
with the ribbons resting on your shoulders,
and you can wander around the house with
a terrible cold and always be prepared for the worst.

I wish I had a photo of my
brilliant 8-year-old self wearing said invention.

Sadly, it never caught on.
The world's loss, I say.

And yes, I am fully aware of what a weird kid I was... No need to point it out.

8½ x 11 page

TWO OF THE MOST IMPORTANT DRIVING forces in human history are invention and innovation—and one of the most amazing things about humanity is that just when you think there can be no new ideas, well … you're wrong. National Inventors' Month takes time to honor the ingenuity that makes the world run.

Every one of us was born with a curious and inventive spirit. Think about the kids in your life, or reflect on memories from your childhood—nothing tops the boundless imagination of children. I've always loved the memory of when I invented the "next big thing," and I wanted to document it so that my children could get a good giggle. (They'll thank me when their mama solves the problem of not having enough tissues when they're sick, too.) I didn't have a photo to accompany this memory, but you know what? I'm glad, in a way. It forced me to think up a way to illustrate my point without one. Necessity is the mother of invention, as they say.

COUNTING PEOPLE IS ONE OF HISTORY'S OLDEST activities. While it might seem like a lot of work—and it is—statistics collected in a census are crucial for identifying where people live and work, projecting growth, and understanding how much tax revenue is necessary to provide services for a population. The first official U.S census occurred in 1790 when the country had just 3.9 million inhabitants.

Bridget, since Daddy and I were born in 1972 the world population has almost doubled from 3.8 billion people to over 6.6 billion—you're about the 6,594,274,993rd

It's a big world out there with a whole lot of people in it, but there's only one YOU.

12 x 12 page

Before Bridget was born, I started thinking about just how many people there are in the world and how that might affect her life as she grows up in the 21st century. I occasionally checked the population clock available at the U.S. Census Bureau's website *(census.gov)* about a month before she was born; then I had the idea that it would be cool to actually know what number she would be in that growing population. (Yes, I'm fully aware that this story is headed into the Kingdom of Complete Nerdiness.) I bookmarked the site and had my family check it after we called home from the hospital with the news that she was born.

August 1, 1876

Colorado Day

12 x 12 spread

COLORADO WAS ADMITTED TO THE UNITED

States as the 38th state in 1876. The United States was just 100 years old, the Wild West was earning its reputation, and the first telephone call had been placed by Alexander Graham Bell just a few months before.

Because of our somewhat transient Air Force lifestyle, all three of my children were born in different states: Wyoming, Colorado, and California. I made this page for Gracie about her birth state of Colorado in honor of the state's admittance to the Union—what better way to celebrate that anniversary? I chose a handful of random, unrelated photos I love from the time we lived there and created a photo collage to show her what a beautiful place Colorado is. I love landscape photography, but my landscape photos don't generally make it into my scrapbooks—this was the perfect opportunity to pull a few in. Check the date your home state was officially admitted and pencil in a special project to honor it. It's nice to remember where we come from!

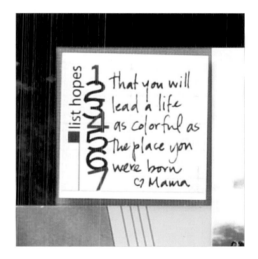

August 15

Julia Child's Birthday

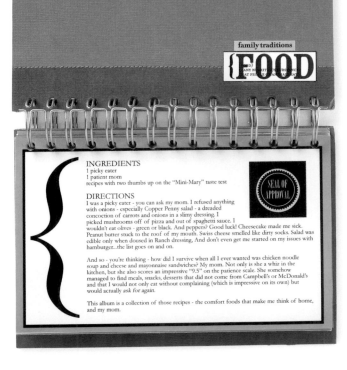

family traditions

{FOOD}

INGREDIENTS
1 picky eater
1 patient mom
recipes with two thumbs up on the "Mini-Mary" taste test

DIRECTIONS
I was a picky eater - you can ask my mom. I refused anything with onions - especially Copper Penny salad - a dreaded concoction of carrots and onions in a slimy dressing. I picked mushrooms off of pizza and out of spaghetti sauce. I wouldn't eat olives - green or black. And peppers? Good luck! Cheesecake made me sick. Peanut butter stuck to the roof of my mouth. Swiss cheese smelled like dirty socks. Salad was edible only when doused in Ranch dressing. And don't even get me started on my issues with hamburger...the list goes on and on.

And so - you're thinking - how did I survive when all I ever wanted was chicken noodle soup and cheese and mayonnaise sandwiches? My mom. Not only is she a whiz in the kitchen, but she also scores an impressive "9.5" on the patience scale. She somehow managed to find meals, snacks, desserts that did not come from Campbell's or McDonald's and that I would not only eat without complaining (which is impressive on its own) but would actually *ask* for again.

This album is a collection of those recipes - the comfort foods that make me think of home, and my mom.

SEAL OF APPROVAL

TIPS: *When compiling a family cookbook you plan to use on a regular basis, try Mary's tips:*

1. *Include a photo of every recipe so that the cook knows what the final product should look like.*

2. *Use a simple recipe card format that can be used for long or short ingredient lists and directions.*

3. *Make the page design flat so it can be laminated later for actual use in the kitchen.*

4. *Create a design scheme that doesn't depend on specific products, so you can add to the book for years to come—even after your embellishments have been discontinued.*

5. *Choose an album with a spiral or three-ring binding so the pages stay open while you cook.*

JULIA CHILD IS AN AMERICAN ICON. HER SENSE of humor and passion for cooking were contagious throughout her 45-year career as a professional chef and TV host. She believed the kitchen should be a family room, perfect for cooking up happy memories shared over homemade food that, above all, tasted good.

Mary had been wanting to compile a special cookbook of her mom's recipes for years. The way she was storing them—scribbled on scraps of paper, jotted in old notebooks, and printed from emails—wasn't conducive to actually cooking from them. So she came up with this album solution, adding quirky quotes by Julia Child directly onto the photos. After all, cooking should be fun, right?

8 x 5½ mini-album

by Mary MacAskill

I was 32 when I started cooking; up until then, I just ate.
- Julia Child -

INGREDIENTS
1 1/2 C. flour
1 1/2 C. rolled oats
1 1/2 C. buttermilk
1 T. baking powder
1/2 t. baking soda
1/2 C. egg substitute
1/2 C. brown sugar
1/3 C. Puritan Oil
1 C. chopped cherries
1 t. almond extract

cherry-almond
muffins

DIRECTIONS
Preheat oven to 400 F. Spray muffin pan with non-stick cooking spray; set aside. In a medium bowl, stir together flour, baking powder, and baking soda. In another bowl, pour buttermilk over oats. Add to flour mixture. In a small bowl, combine egg substitute, brown sugar, oil and almond extract. Pour into flour mixture and gently fold until mixture is moistened. Batter will be lumpy. Spoon into prepared pan and bake for 20 - 25 minutes. Cool 5 minutes. Makes 12 muffins.

The only time to eat diet food
is while you're waiting for the steak to cook.
- Julia Child -

INGREDIENTS
2 Devil's Food cake mixes
1- 1 1/2 C. shortening
4 eggs
8 oz. cream cheese
3 1/2 C. powdered sugar
1/4 C. butter
2 t. vanilla

homemade
oreos

DIRECTIONS
In a bowl, combine cake mixes, eggs, and shortening. Beat well. Roll into nickel-sized balls and place on ungreased cookie sheets. Bake at 350 F for 7-8 minutes. Cookies will look undone and will crack on top. Cool. In a second bowl, mix cream cheese, powdered sugar, butter and vanilla. Beat frosting mixture until smooth, and refrigerate for fifteen minutes. Spread icing on wrong side of cookies and put together like oreos.

I just hate health food.
- Julia Child -

INGREDIENTS
2 T. butter
2 C. coconut
1 8-oz. pkg. cream cheese
2 t. milk
3 1/2 C. powdered sugar
1/2 t. vanilla
1 pkg. yellow cake mix
1 4-oz. pkg. vanilla pudding mix
1 3/4 C. water
4 eggs
1/4 C. oil
2 C. coconut
1 C. chopped walnuts

coconut
cake

DIRECTIONS
Brown coconut in butter. Cool. Mix 1 3/4 C. browned coconut with cream cheese, milk, powdered sugar, and vanilla to make frosting. Set aside. Blend cake mix, pudding mix, water, eggs, and oil. Beat at medium speed for 4 minutes. Stir in coconut and nuts. Pour into 3 greased, floured 9" pans. Bake at 350 F for 35 minutes. Cool 15 minutes. Remove from pan and frost. Sprinkle with remaining coconut.

How can a nation be great
if its bread tastes like Kleenex?
- Julia Child -

INGREDIENTS
3 C. flour
1/2 C. quick oats
1/8 C. brown sugar
1 1/2 t. salt
1 1/2 T. margarine
1/4 C. warm milk
1 1/3 C. warm water
1 pkg. yeast

oatmeal
bread

DIRECTIONS
Allow yeast to reach room temperature. Combine all ingredients in bread machine. Set to dough cycle, and when complete, allow to rest in an 8" loaf pan sprayed with non-stick cooking spray. When dough has doubled in size, bake at 350 F for 25 minutes or until golden.

IF YOU AREN'T FAMILIAR WITH BESPECTACLED American poet Ogden Nash (1902–1971), you're missing out. His light-hearted, witty poetry has been delighting both adults and children for decades. He's the type of writer who makes you feel more creative just by association. So go ahead, give him a read.

I can honestly say that it never would have occurred to me to collect armadillos had I not married into the last name Dillow... but they've been finding their way to me steadily through the years now.

THE ARMADILLO
The armadillo lives inside
a corrugated plated hide
Below the border this useful creature
of tidy kitchens is a feature,
for housewives use an armadillo
to scour their pots,
instead of Brillo. —Ogden Nash

collection est. 1975

12 x 12 page

Shortly after I was married, I found an anthology of quirky poems titled *Ogden Nash's Zoo*. I was thrilled to discover his poem "The Armadillo," which I immediately jotted down on a scrap piece of paper in my purse. Now that I was a Dillow I seemed to be discovering armadillos everywhere, and it only seemed natural to start collecting them! It just shows that inspiration truly is everywhere. Years later it occurred to me that I ought to make a page about my eccentric collection, and I have Mr. Nash to thank for inspiring it.

August 25, 1939

Wizard of Oz Premiere

no place like home april 2007

12 x 12 page

You love your room, sweetpea. It contains music and quiet, history and memories, some very dear monkeys, and a lot of love. Mama

favorite place

FEW MOVIES HAVE CAPTURED THE imagination of so many as *The Wizard of Oz,* based on L. Frank Baum's classic fairy tale, *The Wonderful Wizard of Oz,* published in 1900. Since the film's 1939 premiere, its popularity has remained undiminished, making it the most watched movie of all time.

There are countless ways to be inspired by *The Wizard of Oz* on your pages. I chose one of the more obvious themes, "there's no place like home" as my starting point. I wanted to get Maddie's perspective on this idea, so I asked her what her favorite part of our home was. Her answer, hands down, was her bedroom. We had great fun wandering around her room, taking close-up photos of her prized possessions and everyday furnishings—the things she associates with normalcy, comfort, and love. I put 18 of those photos on my layout, making a colorful mosaic fit for a 4-year-old.

5 x 6 mini-album
by Mary MacAskill

1 to share the spotlight

2 to fall asleep to snoring

3 to love cuddles

4 to have a sidekick

5 to learn to play in the grass

THE ANIMAL MIRACLE FOUNDATION created National Dog Day in order to honor the bond between man (in the non-gender-specific form of the word) and man's best friend. The AMF is a nonprofit organization dedicated to protecting animals from cruelty and neglect, and one goal of National Dog Day is to raise money to help ensure all dogs have a good home.

Mary loves her pugs, two little dogs with personalities so big they easily fill up any room they enter. If you've ever lived with a dog, you know how much energy is invested in that dog's health and happiness. Mary wanted to create a playful mini-album to describe that relationship visually. She loved the chance to play with the vibrant papers and embellishments she chose, and the photos carry her theme without needing much journaling.

DATE
August

EVENT
Most Popular Family
Reunion Time

DID YOU KNOW MORE FAMILY REUNIONS are planned for August than any other time of the year? For scrapbookers, attending a family reunion can be like winning the lottery—hundreds of photo opportunities with people we love, and thousands of stories waiting to be told! Whether your family's reunion happened last week or last century, August is the perfect time to sit down and scrapbook it.

8 x 8 spread
by Laura Kurz

Laura wanted to document this sweet, 40-year-old photo from a family reunion past, so she enlisted her father's help to identify as many people as possible. Even then, it was difficult to come up with everyone's name! Not wanting to give up, Laura simply described the people she couldn't identify by name—which is much better than not mentioning them at all. She kept the right side of her 8 x 8 spread as simple as possible to draw attention to the caption, which also doubles as a clever design element.

1
2
3
4
5
6
7
8
9
10
11
12
13

This month...

wonder about your grandparents before they were grandparents

14

thank your lucky stars for Google

15

reflect on a day we will never forget

16

pay tribute to childhood books you've passed on to your kids

17

revel in a friendship

18

examine the meaning of citizenship

19

chart your unexpected journeys

20

remember a favorite hunting or fishing trip

21

think about what makes a good neighbor

22

let Shel Silverstein be your guide

23

play music, listen to music, be grateful for music

24
25
26
27
28
29
30

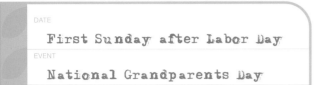

Oh, how I wish I knew the story behind this photo
Grandma Watson
before she was a Grandma
before she was a Watson
circa 1940s

8½ x 11 page

THE NATIONAL GRANDPARENTS DAY Council sponsors National Grandparents Day, an occasion that celebrates the bond between grandparents and their grandchildren. In addition, the organization advocates greater awareness of the nation's elderly population living in nursing homes—most of which are grandparents.

This particular photo of my grandma has always enchanted me. I don't know where it was taken, who took the photo, or how old she was (only that she must have been a teenager or in her early 20s). I often wonder what the people I love were like long ago, and these unanswered questions keep me focused on what's important to share on my pages. Whether you highlight the activities you share, lessons you have learned, or things you wonder about, spend some time honoring your grandparents today!

DATE

September 7, 1998

EVENT

Google Debut

forester arm rest extension
ear infection treatment
girl scout oath
tricycle lyrics
tires tracy california
seville classic laundry sorter
lemon tea benefits

Go gle

{what did I ever do without it?}

Just a one-month random sampling of the 50 gazillion Google searches I've made since its inception in September 1998

drug epidemic portland oregon
top ten shell beaches
stinson beach california
pregnancy nasal congestion remedy
danielle cross spokane
"elizabeth dillow"
little house on the prairie music
magpie
nutcracker kennedy center
louis daguerre
single family homes arlington
babi italia
george mason elementary fairfax
k & company girl scout collection
america the beautiful
jc penney commercial music
forever thursday
luscious jackson
mountain mike's
i have something in my pocket
the last kiss
flag etiquette
mp600 won't print red

8½ x 11 page

DID YOU LEARN THE WORD "GOOGOL" in elementary school? I did, and I thought it was the weirdest thing I'd learned yet in a math class. (How naïve I was back then—I had no idea how weird math would get for me as I progressed through high school!) The word represents the number one followed by 100 zeros, a number too big to comprehend, really. Clever folks that they are, the founders of the world's best search engine named their company "Google"— a play on words that hints at the company's mission, which is to create order out of the infinite amount of information available in cyberspace.

I'm not afraid to admit it: I can't remember what life was like before Google. Not a day goes by that I don't conduct a Google search or two or 50, calling up the information I need with a quick click of the mouse. Because I love lists, I decided to keep track of everything I "Googled" during a one-month period. This is a great way to freeze in time the things you're thinking and wondering about right now. And it's refreshing to take a break from the routine and experiment with a new journaling approach now and then.

YEARS HAVE PASSED SINCE THE EVENTS OF
September 11, 2001, but the memories of that day are still fresh
in my mind—and if history is any indication, they will remain that
way for the rest of my life. Some historical events simply burn
themselves into memory. Ask anyone who was of "remembering
age" in 1963 what they were doing when they learned that
President Kennedy had been assassinated, and you'll see this
simple fact in action: some things you just don't forget.

Maddie hadn't been born yet in September 2001, but being
pregnant with her at that time impacted my perspective of the
tragic day's events. Now as a parent, I truly struggle with what
the world holds for her. The reason I finally sat down and
created this album for Maddie was my realization that the
tragedies and challenges in the world won't wait for her—or
anyone—to be ready for them. What we *can* do is acknowledge
the events and remember the stories of sacrifice and courage.
If you look beyond the fun of pretty paper and trendy
embellishments, scrapbooking can be a powerful way
to explore your reactions to difficult events.

TIP: *If you decide to tackle a September 11 album of your own,
take a little pressure off. Decide up front to limit your product
choices so the story becomes the focus above all else, as it should.*

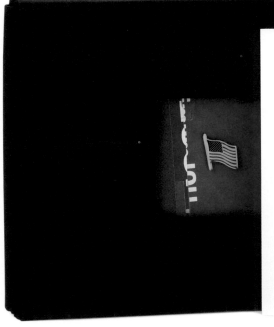

6 x 6 mini-album

Dear Maddie,

I want to tell you a story about something real, something that
happened in our country before you were born but soon after I
learned you would be born. It is a story about two skyscrapers in
New York City, my memories of the most awful day for the United
States in my lifetime, and a book about a man named Philippe Petit.
I'm not sure how old you will be when I'm ready to share this story
with you—it's a terribly scary one, with repercussions that color the
world you were born into. It's a story that starkly divides history in
our country into before and after. It's a story that you absolutely
must know as an American even though it is an unhappy one. I've
always been interested in the details of things that happened before I
was born, and I know you are, too. I hope it will inspire you to
learn and consider your role in this world.

Love, Mama

The World
Trade Center
1986

Before you were born—in fact, just before I was born—two buildings were built in New York City. In 1970, the first building of the World Trade Center Complex was completed (1 World Trade Center, North Tower) and in 1972, the year I was born, the second building was completed (2 World Trade Center, South Tower). Both buildings were 110 floors and until 1973, were the tallest buildings in the world. The Sears Tower replaced them as the world's tallest building when it was constructed in Chicago. They were a symbol of capitalism in the U.S. as over 50,000 people worked there and another 200,000 passed through on business each day. The complex was so big it had its own zip code. When I was in 7th grade, I had the chance to visit the public observation deck of the South Tower when I was in New York City for a jazz band trip. I remember it was windy with a remarkable view of the city, but I don't remember much else. I wish I had paid more attention.

7:00 am
World History
Central HS

Fast forward to the fall of 2001. Daddy and I were living in Cheyenne, Wyoming. I had just started teaching American History and World History at Cheyenne Central High School and East High School and found out that I was pregnant with you.

On the morning of September 11, I went to school at 6:30 am just like normal, and welcomed my 7:00 am World History class at Central just like normal. It was a small group of students that I got to know quickly; none of us were particularly early morning people, but all of us had committed to being there for a variety of reasons so we had a relatively easy time of it building a community. These are the people I bought an extra hour of "normal" with, an extra hour of "before." While we were in that classroom discussing ancient world history, disaster struck. We didn't know it until the door opened again at 7:50 am, but while we were in that Mountain Standard Time classroom, two hijacked airplanes crashed into the North and South Towers of the World Trade Center. Soon after a hijacked plane crashed into the Pentagon. A fourth hijacked plane would eventually crash in a field in Pennsylvania, foiled by passengers who acted to wrestle control away from the hijackers.

THE TOWERS

MORDICAI GERSTEIN

The book
we read
together

Which leads me to Philippe Petit. Somehow I never learned about Philippe Petit until this year, 2006. He is a French tightrope walker who in 1974, rigged a wire between the two towers of the World Trade Center and managed to walk back and forth until he was caught and surrendered himself to arrest. His story is absolutely amazing, and if it weren't for you I might still not know it. You see, this fall you picked out a book named *The Man Who Walked Between the Towers* by Mordicai Gerstein on your quest to choose Caldecott books at the Livermore Public Library. I had never heard of it and so didn't know what to expect. It was such a powerful story that I was unable to finish, so overcome with tears I was trying not to let you see. It ended so simply, though. "Now the towers are gone. But in memory, as if imprinted on the sky, the towers are still there. And part of that memory is the joyful morning, August 7, 1974, when Philippe Petit walked between them on the air."

I didn't cry as much the day it happened as I did after reading this book to you.

DATE

September 13

EVENT

Roald Dahl Day

8½ x 11 page

by Margaret Scarbrough

A READING TRADITION

Ahh Hoonie, you've finally gotten to the age where you will actually sit down for a moment or two while we read you a book. You'll take the time to finger the pictures, smile at your favorite parts and even help us turn the page on occasion. What a joy it is to see you at this stage. Where books start holding some meaning for you. Did you know that you actually come from a family of big readers? And early ones too. (No pressure, of course!) Right now, we're just enjoying you enjoying your books. And who knows, maybe you'll even keep the tradition of Roald Dahl books alive. Both Matthew and I began pretty early with his stuff. In fact, *James and the Giant Peach* was Matthew's first chapter book and *Danny the Champion of the World* was one of mine. I'm thinking of holding *Charlie and the Chocolate Factory* in reserve for you. Then again, you may decide to choose something else. Something by a different author, even. Either way, I'm just happy knowing that we've got you started on the reading path. May books always hold a special place in your heart (even if it is just *Busy Monkeys* right now).

TIP: *Don't forget the details. When you take a picture of your child reading his or her favorite book, also snap a few extra photos for context, such as a close-up shot of the bookshelves or a special basket where you store favorite titles.*

THERE AREN'T MANY

characters in children's literature more endearing than Charlie Bucket, Veruca Salt, Willy Wonka, and the rest of the crew from *Charlie and the Chocolate Factory*—unless you get acquainted with Matilda, or James, or the Big Friendly Giant. Simply put, Welsh author Roald Dahl's distinguished writing career produced books so brilliant that they've become instant classics, guaranteed to pass from one generation to the next.

Margaret's solo reading career began with a stack of books recommended by her father's co-worker, since her father—an immigrant from Korea—was unfamiliar with American children's literature. She's thankful for that serendipitous exchange, because her father purchased everything on the list, including a whole slew of Roald Dahl titles. After reading *Danny the Champion of the World,* Margaret was hooked. When her son Matthew was old enough for his first chapter book, a tradition was born, and when Hoonie is ready, a Roald Dahl classic will be waiting for him, too. It's little connections like these that strengthen our family histories. Be sure to set some time aside this month to document the little things that have been passed from generation to generation (and for what reason) in your own family.

DATE

Third Sunday in

September

EVENT

National Women's

Friendship Day

one who you forget lives 1,500 miles away instead of on the next street over

one who has seen what you look like after a long day at band camp

one who can talk you out of resigning after a particularly bad day

everyone should have a friend like this

one who knows you inside and out

Kattie Novak Spies
friends since 1986

8½ x 11 page

IN 1999, KAPPA DELTA SORORITY founded National Women's Friendship Day—a day for women to honor the friends that enrich and sustain them. What better way to celebrate your closest female friends—be they neighbors, college roommates, childhood pals, or even relatives—than to immortalize the relationship on a scrapbook page?

My friend Kattie and I met at a youth group picnic in middle school, and after more than 20 years of friendship we don't know what we'd do without each other. She is my confidante, my substitute for therapy on bad days, my cheerleader on good ones, and while we haven't seen each other in 10 years, she's just a phone call away anytime I need her. I made this page as much for my daughters as for me. One of my great hopes for Maddie, Gracie, and Bridget is that they will each have a friendship like this. I want them to know from an early age that good friends are essential to a happy existence.

12 x 12 page
by Anna Aspnes

A desire to belong somewhere but torn between two worlds.

Raised in the United Kingdom and daughter of a Royal Air Force Officer, who would have thought I'd be raising my own children under the protective wings of the United States Air Force? Certainly not I. It was never my intention but it was my choice.

Over the past 9 years I have struggled with being labelled an "alien" resident, without the rights or privileges that citizenship brings. Granted in the beginning I did not deserve such privileges. I was determined to support Eric in his military career to my best ability while remaining true to my British roots and I admit that I did fall short. Now that I am raising 2 American citizens I see how important it is that they take pride in their own roots with a genuine passion for their people and surroundings.

I believe that much of a country's strength is derived from it's people and their belief in their land, their customs and their very being. This belief is so great that those men and women who join our military services are willing die for our liberties and privileges. That is their pledge and was both my Dad's, my sister's and my husband's pledge when they joined their respective services

So where does that leave me? I am torn and there is an overwhelming feeling of guilt. While I now find comfort in the familiarity of the United States, the place I call home, how do I tell the man who raised me and served for 35 years, that I want to take that final step, one that in essence turns my back on his country and on everything I was taught to believe in? Or am I making too much of this? I am still me regardless of where my citizenship lies.

I just know it's not easy walking the fine line between two worlds, neither recognizing the place in which I raised nor fully being part of the place where I live now. The truth is I just want to belong... (February 24, 2007)

IN 1952, PRESIDENT HARRY TRUMAN signed a bill establishing September 17 as Citizenship Day. The idea was to honor both native-born and foreign-born citizens of the United States, celebrating their accomplishments, rights, and responsibilities.

Born and raised in the United Kingdom, Anna now lives in a household full of American citizens. That daily dichotomy often causes her to reflect upon her position in the world. After so many years of living the American life and raising her American children, she wonders if the time has come to make her feelings of being settled in her adopted country a bit more official—by applying for U.S. citizenship. Citizenship isn't just an abstract concept, but a concrete set of defining beliefs and characteristics. By putting these thoughts down on paper, Anna can help her children one day understand the unique experience their mum felt straddling two worlds.

DATE

September 18, 1947

EVENT

United States

Air Force Established

8½ x 11 spread

I sent 119 Christmas cards this year.
73 of those Christmas cards went to people I know because of the Air Force.

This little statistic that occurred to me as I was sealing my cards up really floored me. 73 families that I wouldn't know had it not been for our somewhat transient lifestyle: first Montana, then Wyoming, then Colorado... places I likely never would have lived had it not been for Matt's military service. 73 families who have made my life so much richer, so much more meaningful, and have been so vital to my happiness. It really got me thinking about how different my life has been because of the Air Force: richer, fuller, and just a little adventurous.

I really had no idea what was in store for me when Matt received his commission in 1994. I stayed contentedly put in the same town for 18 years, only to attend college some 4 1/2 hours away in the same state. Ohio was home to me, and had I not begun dating Matt, probably would have remained home to me. Though there is a genetic disposition towards wanderlust among my maternal side of the family, I would venture to say that it skipped me entirely. Montana, Wyoming, and Colorado were distant lands whose beauty did not beckon me in any physical sense; I admired photos in National Geographic and other photography books, but it never occurred to me to pick up and go live there.

But life can change in an instant.

Once that commission was in hand—and shortly thereafter an engagement ring, too—my life changed. I didn't realize it at the time, but I was about to begin a series of life experiences that were sometimes small, sometimes huge, but always surreal in a way. The first of these experiences is almost laughably mundane: I remember sitting in a McDonald's in Kalispell, Montana in 1995 on the way home from a speech tournament thinking to myself: "Oh my goodness, how weird is it that I am sitting in a restaurant in Kalispell, Montana with Tim and Mike, a speech coach myself, responsible for the well-being of all these high school kids so far from home? Who would have ever thought??" I remember standing at the peak of Red Mountain with Matt and Jill experiencing sheer astonishment that I had climbed to the top of a mountain nearly 2000 miles from my childhood home. I remember driving with Amy to book club in Fort Collins, thinking to myself how utterly unbelievable it was that I was a member of a book club in Fort Collins, Colorado—a place I had never heard of just a few years before. I had a baby in a hospital room that overlooked the state capitol building in Cheyenne, and another at Fort Carson. Because of the Air Force, I found Playgroup and wonderful women I can't imagine living without. Since those early years away from Ohio, I've had hundreds of these moments where I stop in disbelief at how amazing it is that life turns out the way it does. I've built my own support systems and set down my roots in three communities so far, full of people who have encouraged me, laughed with me, and guided me through difficult times. I can't imagine what my life would be like had I stayed in Ohio after graduation. I'm sure it would have been rich in different ways, with different people and a different path. But there's a part of me who thanks my lucky stars that I didn't have to miss these people I've met along the way, who thanks my lucky stars for the opportunity to adopt these friends and their hometowns as my own, if only for a while.

There is also a part of me that is dreading the next move. Moving means leaving, transitioning from every day or every week to long distance or once a year or never again. The finality of moving weighs hard on me, because now that I've moved enough times I know that while you can go back and visit, life is different by the time you get there again. But for the many reasons to appreciate Matt's service: duty to country, a vision of peace through deterrence, and individual integrity, no list would be complete without adding the people. The Air Force life has given me people to love and to experience life with. For that I am eternally grateful.

MORE THAN 1.4 MILLION MEN AND women serve on active duty in the five branches of the military in the United States, many with families whose lives are influenced daily by the rhythm of military life. The newest branch of the military, the United States Air Force, was formed as an independent branch on September 18, 1947.

Looking back over the first half of my "career" as a military spouse, I see how priceless the experience has been. On the anniversary of the establishment of the branch of service that has influenced my life so profoundly, I wanted to describe that influence—for me now, for me in the future—as a reminder to look at the big picture. How has the military affected your life?

Fourth Saturday of September

National Hunting

and Fishing Day

IN ORDER TO PROMOTE THE BENEFITS of the time spent outdoors, President Richard Nixon signed a proclamation in 1972 that designated the fourth Saturday in September as National Hunting and Fishing Day.

5 x 7 mini-album
by Anna Aspnes

Because of her husband's Air Force career, Anna has lived all over the world—and their time in Alaska (where they live now) has been rich with dramatic landscapes and the splendor of the great outdoors. Her family's trip to Homer, Alaska, the halibut fishing capital of the world, is documented in this little book, which feels as much like a nature sketch journal as it does a scrapbook. By starting with photography that tells the whole story—not just the fish caught, but the surroundings, people, and mood of the trip—and adding a simple color scheme and style that complements the setting, she captured everything that's good and fun about the sport.

DATE

Fourth Sunday in September

EVENT

National Good Neighbor Day

neighbors

melissa & elizabeth · 6/06

a good neighbor bakes you goodies
and invites you over for coffee or Dr. Pepper

a good neighbor sits in the driveway with
you for hours while your children play

a good neighbor is happy to go to the Farmers'
Market with you, early in the morning

a good neighbor doesn't hesitate to toss you
her housekeys and her youngest child
when the other one breaks her arm
(she knows you would do the same)

a good neighbor reassures you that you are
doing OK on the hard days and even
better on the good ones

a good neighbor doesn't mind coming
over at 10:00 pm to help you vacuum
the night before you close on your house

8½ x 11 page

NATIONAL GOOD NEIGHBOR DAY WAS founded in 1971 on the simple principle that "good neighbors make a happy world." The relationship between neighbors is different from any other because a good neighbor is not just a family member, friend, or colleague, but a mixture of all three. The National Good Neighbor Foundation urges everyone to pitch in and help in their communities, strengthening neighborhoods everywhere.

I've never met a better neighbor than Melissa, who showed up on our doorstep the first week we moved in with cookies and offers of friendship. Three years later, when we were moving once again, she was there with broom and vacuum to help me get the house ready for its new owners. That is the dictionary definition of neighborly! I miss my good neighbor and wanted to pay tribute to her by recording some of the highlights of our three years on the cul-de-sac together. It's important to include all the people you love in your scrapbooks!

DATE

September 25

EVENT

Shel Silverstein's Birthday

8½ x 11 spread
by Mi'Chelle Larsen

SPEND A MINUTE IN THE WORLD

created by Shel Silverstein—one populated by boa constrictors, dancing pants, Hungry Mungry, monsters, cows, hammocks, and more—and you know you've entered a magical place. Most famous for his many collections of children's poetry, Silverstein was also a composer, lyricist, and author for adults. His unique perspective, humor, and excitement for life are contagious. For the record, these are characteristics I love in a good scrapbook page, too.

Mi'Chelle looked to Silverstein for a little thematic inspiration in the creation of this page about her brother, Chandler, and his quirky habit of collecting "stuff" when he was little. The page came together in under an hour, which Mi'Chelle says is a miracle since she's been known to push things around on paper for days before she'll commit to a design. When you've got good inspiration, though, things just come together quickly! Chandler was always known as a bit of a "Hector the Collector" growing up, so it only seemed natural to spell it out in cute "junk."

DATE

September

EVENT

National Piano Month

8½ x 11 page

I'm not sure I've ever properly thanked my parents for one of their greatest gifts to me

The opportunity to play piano

They paid for years of lessons — dropped me off and picked me up each week

without complaint

made sure I practiced for a half hour every day, even when I didn't want to

let me quit for two years in high school until I realized I couldn't live without it

paid to store the old avocado green upright until I could move it to Montana

helped pay for the replacement a few years ago

I'm not all that good anymore

I peaked my freshman year of college

but that isn't really the point

January 2006

TIP: *Don't be afraid to attempt a "train of thought" layout, where you simply communicate something that's been on your mind. You probably have plenty of "event" and "moments" layouts, but it's equally important to scrapbook the things you think about.*

THE NATIONAL PIANO FOUNDATION celebrates National Piano Month each September as a way to encourage the study of piano—a pursuit that has far-reaching benefits. Piano playing strengthens fine motor skills, assists in cognitive development, and can even make you better at math. But the joy of being able to make music is often reward enough, all on its own.

I started playing piano in second grade, taking lessons every Tuesday for years. I never had ambitions to play in front of large crowds as a concert pianist; I wanted to play just for the sake of playing. I'm often grateful for my parents' willingness to shuttle me to my lessons each week, because playing the piano has been a lifelong joy—something I wanted to share with my family in this layout.

October

1

2

3

4

5

6

7

8

9

10

11

12

This month... 13

be aware 14

display a family legacy, however small 15

send joy through the mail 16

examine a life influenced by books 17

define your world 18

tell what time means to you 19

consider why character matters 20

log some game time 21

22

23

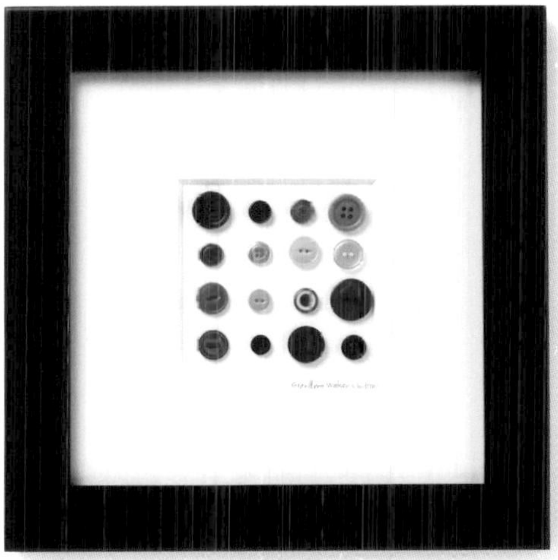

24

25

26

27

28

29

30

31

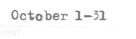

6 x 6 mini-album

Carol
Katie
Camille
Helen
Kattie

it's not just a walk

Sure, it's a two day, 39 mile walk for breast cancer. But it is so much more than a charity walk. For months you give up every Saturday and walk in the rain, heat, cold and sun. Your team becomes an extension of your family. As the training walks lengthen from two hours to four to six, they begin to know more and more about you. Questions like "how did you meet your husband?" and "guess what my kids did this week?" will lead to sharing intimate details about your life. And at some point, you will begin to talk about cancer.

TIP: *Don't forget the power of a scrapbook as a gift!*

ON YOUR NEXT ROAD TRIP, TRY THIS LITTLE exercise in perspective: reset your trip odometer and see how far 39 miles is. That, my friends, is the distance of the Avon Walk, which is held in locations throughout the country each year to raise money for breast cancer research. That's no stroll in the park. That's a serious trek.

I'm so proud of my friend Kattie. She participated in the Avon Walk in Charlotte, North Carolina, on two separate occasions, logging hundreds of training miles to prepare for each year's walk (not to mention the nearly 80 miles she covered during the actual events!). I wanted to celebrate her passionate commitment to this cause with more than just my financial donation, so I decided to make a simple gift album commemorating her achievement (and the achievement of her walking partners). The mini-album I created wasn't a surprise, but rather a long-distance collaboration: she agreed to send me photos and answer my many questions about her experience. I organized her answers into narrative form, pairing them with photographs that fit.

official gear

it's about something more

When cancer becomes the topic of conversation, you will talk about how it has touched you. Why you are doing this walk. Soon comes fundraising, letter-writing, and publicity. People begin to share emails, write letters, and send pictures of loved ones who are fighting or have lost the battle to breast cancer. And once those conversations begin, you realize that this is what the walk is all about. Getting the message out. Helping women become aware of their bodies. Strengthening us for the future.

LOVE

this walk is for her

I have walked for the past two years in honor of many friends and family who have suffered the effects of breast cancer. And although that is a large part of why I participate, I will keep on participating for Mia. With Jeff's family history, I feel as if I need to do as much as I can to find a cure. This walk is a start. She is only two. What will the world of science and research discover about her generation's risk for breast cancer?

be aware

this walk is worthwhile

We walked 39.3 miles on October 21-22, 2006 and helped the Avon Foundation raise over $1.6 million to contribute to breast cancer research and care. The Carolinas Medical Center received $250,000 to assist Mecklenburg County Breast Care Management programs. Palmetto Health Foundation in Columbia, South Carolina received $250,000 towards the cost of a new digital mammography machine. The North Carolina Baptist Hospital in Winston-Salem received $125,000 to help in the creation of a new community outreach program. The Presbyterian Cancer Center in Charlotte received $125,000 to support the expansion of community outreach and patient services in Mecklenburg County and eleven surrounding counties. This walk is worthwhile.

10 x 10 frame

DATE

October 1-31

EVENT

Family History Month

FAMILY HISTORY MONTH IS CELEBRATED every October by local and regional genealogical societies that are passionate about preserving the past. "Genealogy" may sound like an intimidating word, but thanks to new technologies, it's getting easier and easier to trace family histories and uncover stories about our ancestors.

Can a scrapbook be framed and hung on a wall? You bet! I've always loved the big tin of buttons that belonged to my Grandma Watson. An old button collection is a small legacy to possess, but it's a priceless bit of family history at the same time. I have terrific memories of playing with the button tin when I was little, and I wanted

a way to display a few of them in a nice decor piece that will hang in a place of honor in my home. When I was finished, I thought it would be good to provide a bit of context for anyone curious enough to look at the back of the frame— the story about the buttons can be found there. The entire project took me less than an hour—a little more if you count the frames I created for my mom and sisters as Christmas gifts. Do you have family treasures you could display in a frame or shadowbox?

A Little History

Grandma Watson kept her buttons in a metal cookie tin and I remember how much I loved it when she brought them out from wherever it was she kept them in her house on Linway. (The Pink Room? The Blue Room? The attic?) I liked digging my little hands into all that color, and picking out my favorites only to toss them back in the tin for next time. I still wonder how in the world she managed to collect so many, because there were thousands of them in that tin. Did people used to cut them off when their clothes wore out? Were people unwittingly walking around buttonless, victims of Grandma's scissors! To be honest, I still wonder about that. These buttons are a legacy of color and memory, one that I'm excited to share with my own daughters.

4½ x 7 label on back of frame

First Saturday in October

World Card Making Day

PAPER CRAFTS MAGAZINE, A SISTER PUBLICATION to *Simple Scrapbooks* magazine, established World Card Making Day in 2006 as a way to kick off the busiest card-making season of the year.

Mary put a simple scrapbooking spin on the day by creating a gift album filled with handmade cards. She made a card for each month of the year, sticking to a basic design scheme for all of the cards, varying only the seasonal colors and accents. Mary wanted to create something that could still be useful after the cards were sent, so it doubles as a photo album: once a card is removed, a photo can be added in its place behind the transparency. Brilliant!

VARIATIONS: *Instead of making monthly cards, print words like "joy," "cheer," and "peace" on each pocket, then the recipient can add holiday photos to create a quick Christmas album. Or, create a brag book for grandparents—just leave the pockets empty and send a photo card each month for them to slip into their album.*

8 x 5 mini-album
by Mary MacAskill

I READ FOR:

challenge

escape

story

memory

adventure

inspiration

imagination

possibility

perspective

2½ x 7 bookmarks

escape

Discovering Harry Potter was like rediscovering the part of me that can get lost in books, unwilling to come up for air or lunch or bed.

FRONT

Dear Mr. Potter,

We are pleased to inform you that you have been accepted at Hogwarts School of Witchcraft and Wizardry. Please find enclosed a list of all necessary books and equipment. Term begins on September 1. We await your owl no later than July 31.

Yours sincerely,
Minerva McGonagall

BACK

story

There's just something about this story that I absolutely love. While I have nothing in common with any of the characters each time I read this— and I've read it a lot— I connect to their saga in a very personal way. It is a mysterious, magical story.

FRONT

"I want to tell you a story. It's a strange story. It doesn't have an ending. But you might find it interesting anyway."
— Davita Chandal

BACK

THE NATIONAL BOOK FOUNDATION IS DEVOTED to promoting great American literature and authors. It awards the prestigious National Book Award each year and sponsors outreach and education programs throughout the year, especially during October. The foundation began recognizing each year's best American literature in 1950, and since that time has encouraged winning authors and finalists to share the books that changed their lives.

After reading some of my favorite authors' essays about the books that affected them, I knew I had to make my own list. (Of course, being a scrapbooker, a plain old list wouldn't cut it—hence the bookmarks.) I believe wholeheartedly in the power of reading to transform lives, and I believe that what I read and why I read provides insight about me that can't be discovered anywhere else. I would give my right arm to know what books my ancestors read and loved, what books changed them, and why. I want to preserve this information for someone who might be curious about me in the future.

Tip: Sometimes it's fun to break out of traditional page sizes and try something new. Bookmark sleeves (I bought mine online at craftsuppliesforless.com) hold plenty of possibilities for unique projects. The durable plastic and multiple sizes make them ideal for bookmarks, of course, but they're also great for small scrapbooks for children, handy brag books to throw in a purse or diaper bag, or convenient pockets for collecting receipts and other ephemera while on vacation.

FRONT

BACK

FRONT

BACK

October 16

Dictionary Day

3 x 8½ hanging mini-album
by Margaret Scarbrough

Hoon•ie•ache | *n.* **1** what everyone has in this household by 8:00 pm **2** or after a particularly trying napping session

Hoon•ie•kins | *n.* **1** nickname for Hoonie when he is being especially charming **2** or especially cute

Hoon•er•cise | *v.* **1** what Hoonie is doing when zipping around in his walker **2** or when we hold his hands

OCTOBER 16 IS THE BIRTHDAY of Noah Webster, father of the American dictionary. To honor his contributions to the language, plan a project that celebrates the words that define your world!

Do you make up words in your house that just seem to define a situation or person better than any real word could? Margaret and her husband Jack do all the time—especially when it comes to referring to their son Wesley Owen, better known to the world as Hoonie (a nickname originating from his Korean name, Kwang Hoon). This sweet, funny mini-album serves as a custom-made dictionary, defining Hoonie and his adventures perfectly. Margaret loved using such a diverse mix of patterned papers in her mini-album, which features tiny black-and-white photos throughout.

DATE

October 24

EVENT

Take Back Your Time Day

free time = imagination time spend your time wisely your time is precious take the time to be present

january april july october

february ember

11 12 1
Maddie—
You are almost five years old.
I almost done with preschool, and so
looking forward to kindergarten in the
fall... he could get very busy for you — we
already know kids who have a different activity
every day of the week. Daddy and I believe very
strongly in protecting your free time. Though
it's not that we're going to keep you from
activities — don't worry, you'll still take piano
lessons like you've been wanting for, plus
swimming or whatever — but you will also
have a whole lot of time on your
hands. Time to be a kid.
10 2
9 3
8 4
7 5
6

march ember ember

and now, a few words about your time.

12 x 12 page

EVER WONDERED HOW IN THE WORLD you'll make it through the week with all the activities, meetings, and other commitments cluttering your calendar? Then you might need to take back your time! Visit *timeday.org* and find out how you—with the help of the Take Back Your Time organization—can challenge the epidemic of overwork and over-scheduling that jeopardizes the time you spend with your family and friends, and even threatens your health and peace of mind.

I created this page to remind both Maddie and myself that, as she begins elementary school, we will not fall into the trap of doing so much that we never have time to simply be. I love the recommendation from Take Back Your Time to create non-negotiable windows of time to engage in slow, refreshing activities with family members. Not quick conversations held only during the time spent driving from Point A to Point B, but dinners at the table or game nights or couch-flopping for a movie together. As we enter this new phase in our lives where school leads to the pressure to participate in every activity under the sun, we need to remember that we have the power to control how we spend our time. How can you take back some of your time this month?

8½ x 11 page

THE CHARACTER COUNTS INITIATIVE promotes the "six pillars of character"—trustworthiness, respect, responsibility, fairness, caring, and citizenship. By presidential proclamation, it is celebrated in schools, local communities, and non-profit agencies throughout the United States in late October each year.

I want my daughters to be young women of character. Since we're about to enter a new phase in our family—the one where we send Maddie out in the world to school—I decided to write down a few of the things we're trying to teach her about what good character looks like. I loved the design of a newsletter I picked up at Powell's in Portland, so I decided to put that bold, simple design to work for the bold, simple message of the page. The journaling isn't particularly private, but I like how the folded journaling card serves as a design element—it has just the right splash of color to balance the "black and white" points of character on the page.

September—December

Million Minute

Family Challenge

11 x 8½ page
by Margaret Scarbrough

GAMER

You are a gamer...*in the totally old-fashioned sense of the word.* When you were around three or four, we started a weekly tradition of playing card/board games every Friday night (aka "game night" around here). It was something that we could all look forward to at the end of the week. It didn't take much prep, really, just a few snacks and drinks...*and pajamas were pretty much standard dress.* We'd usually pick about three or four games to play and cheating was always allowed (as long as it was *in your favor, of course). Fast forward a couple years... Hoonie is born and we slowly let game night slide. I know how it happened—we're just all so much busier now—but I'm still not happy about it. After finding these fun pictures, though, I'm thinking that maybe we need to rethink things a bit. That maybe we all need something to look forward to again on Friday nights. Especially since our lives are busier than ever before. How about it, anyone game?

(pictures taken Friday 03/04/05)

THE MILLION MINUTE FAMILY CHALLENGE is organized each year by game manufacturer Patch Products to encourage greater family interaction through the joy of game-playing. Between September and December, individuals or groups simply log their game-playing minutes on the event's website (*millionminute.com*), with each counting toward the collective goal of one million minutes. States compete against each other for the lead, supplying a bit of suspense as the competition heats up. But in the end, it's the individual families—who take time to slow down and enjoy each other's company—that win.

In the Scarbrough household, Family Game Night used to be a regularly scheduled activity until a new baby entered the fray. Coming across these photos of her son Matthew intent on winning a game (of course!) made Margaret yearn for the days where they spent their Friday-night minutes enjoying snacks and games. Isn't it great how scrapbooking can refocus our attention and help us recognize the parts of our lives that are most important?

1
2
3
4
5
6
7
8
9
10
11
12
13
14
15
16
17
18
19
20
21
22
23
24
25
26
27
28
29
30

resemblance

We recently came across this photo of my great uncle Frankie, sometime in his twenties during the 1950s. The resemblance tore him to senior Ryan (right side at his high school graduation in 2005) is almost unbelievable.

Frankie was Ryan's great uncle as well (he was our grandmother Mary's brother). We never met our great uncle Frankie, he caused away suddenly in his forties, but I'm sure he would have loved to see the resemblance in his great nephew.

family

November 5

Guy Fawkes Night/Bonfire Night

12 x 12 spread

by Anna Aspnes

So many fond memories of making Guy Fawkes at school with crumpled-up newspaper and and old *nylons* (hose). There were always many a Guy Fawkes competition, with the prize *"guy"* being chosen for the top of the bonfire. I don't remember if I ever won, but I really enjoyed making them, giving the "guy" a face, and dressing him in old clothes. I even went so far as giving mine old shoes, not to be outdone by anyone. The guy making really was a big deal.

Aside from that, my mum was a stickler for the 7pm bedtime rule, so to be able to stay up anything past that, was very cool, and then there were the sparklers...who doesn't love them? Back then they were like the forbidden fruit, and still are. Mum sadly doesn't have any photos of this favourite celebration, so I have found some unrestricted stock images on-line (You have got to love the internet :) to help visualize my recollections. She remembers dark, cold and wet Bonfire nights, to which she dreaded taking us. Hence, the camera was the last thing on her mind. It's funny how such weather doesn't seem to bother us as children. I only remember mum dressing us in snow suits, on one occasion, and the warming of our fingers around a cup of thick greenpea soup accompanied by the traditional *banger* a.k.a. the English version of the *hotdog* was, I am sure, on this night, particularly comforting.

Much of my childhood was spent on a RAF camp so Bonfire night was a base-wide event with impressive fire works by all accounts. My favorite were definitely the pin or *Cathrine Wheels* as we used to call them. I recently found out these are so called after a popular British candy and consist of a long lace of *Bassetts Liquorice* coiled around an *Allsort*. I wrote about them in a letter to me Granparents back in 1981 (left).

It wasn't until I went to University in Leeds, that I was able to go to a more traditional and low-key village bonfire. In my case, it was *"down Meadowgate"*, the street close to #256 which is where my Grandparents (Davies) lived. It was uneventful, but did have that hometown local feel to it, as well as Parkin, a sticky ginger cake made with black treacle and oatmeal. I remember asking my Grandma for the recipe but then changing my mind, thinking when would I be able to make Parkin at University? Now clearly a BIG bummer!

REMEMBER, REMEMBER THE FIFTH OF NOVEMBER. So starts an English nursery rhyme that teaches about Guy Fawkes and his rather gruesome role in English history. He was one of 13 men who, in the year 1605, plotted to blow up the English Parliament and force King James I from the throne, but he was caught, tortured, and executed instead. The event is still celebrated throughout the United Kingdom by the burning of Guy Fawkes in effigy at big bonfires complete with fireworks and sparklers.

Since Anna's American-born children aren't able to participate in Bonfire Night celebrations, Anna created a layout that recalls a favorite tradition from her childhood so her kids will grow up with a rudimentary knowledge of this very English holiday. She slipped a letter she wrote to her grandmother when she was young into a pocket on her right-hand page. Don't overlook little treasures like this if you have them (but remember to spray them with Archival Mist first).

DATE

November 10, 1969

EVENT

Sesame Street Premiere

8½ x 11 page
by Laura Kurz

When my parents moved to Connecticut before I was born, they were fortunate to befriend a man named Ray Sipherd. He was a writer for Sesame Street, and I'm not sure there was anything cooler to three and four year old me. That was all topped off by a visit to the set in the early 1980s. I'm pictured here at Big Bird's nest with Susan, one of the main characters. I remember very little, except how overwhelming the entire experience was!

SESAME STREET, PRODUCED BY the non-profit organization Sesame Workshop, was created by Jim Henson in 1969 and has since become one of the longest-running television shows in the United States. More than 30 versions of the show are in existence throughout the world, each aiming to inspire, teach, and entertain preschoolers (and adults). Generations of American children grew up watching the groundbreaking show, and that adds up to a lot of *Sesame Street* memories.

Oh, what I would have given to have been in Laura's shoes as a little girl—a real-live visit to the set of the show where she rubbed shoulders with a *Sesame Street* celebrity! Laura's photo and memory of her visit with Susan, aka Dr. Loretta Long, is more than just a happy memory— it's a little piece of American history she'll want to share with future generations. Do you have a favorite character or memory from Sesame Street (or another TV show)? Write it down—your children will love reading about your feelings for something they already love.

Sunny Day

Sunny day—sweepin' the clouds away,
On my way to where the air is sweet.
Can you tell me how to get,
how to get to Sesame Street?

Come and play, everything's A-OK
Friendly neighbors there, that's where we meet
Can you tell me how to get,
how to get to Sesame Street?

—Sesame Street theme song

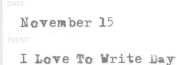
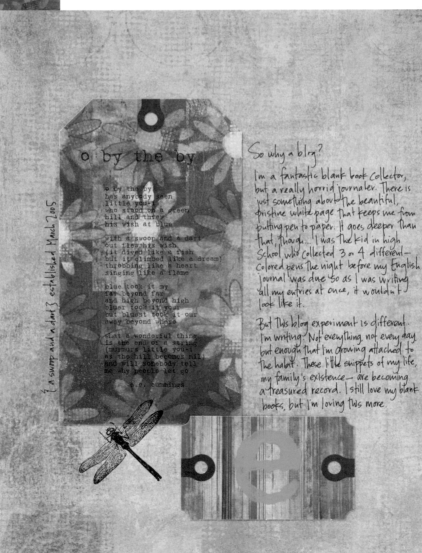

8½ x 11 album

I LOVE TO WRITE DAY IS A LITTLE-KNOWN occasion that encourages people of all ages to sit down and write something—a poem, an essay, a story, journaling for a scrapbook page, you name it! Writing is a challenging activity but one that is rewarding, revealing, and worthwhile. The more you write, the easier it is to put thoughts to paper, so why not take the time to write something today?

title page

Flashback Friday: The Bösendorfer Story

April 7, 2006

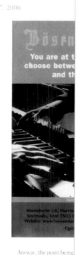

You are at t
choose betwe
and th

Bösendorfer UK, Hurst
Sevenoaks, Kent TN13 1
Website: www.bösender

Anyway, the point being

So when I sat down to p
It made me nervous, but
now, but I do remember
panic

A Bösendorfer Imperial

Normal pianos have 88

Information that would

blog entries

Prunehilde

November 5, 2005

Dear Gracie,

Despite the fact that you

crawled into the dishwasher this week

were eating fistfuls of dirt out of the ivy planter yesterday when I was helping Maddie

don't take drinking out of a cup seriously

don't understand the word NO (even though you know 9 signs now)

spit your food at me when you're done

try to jump out of your highchair

act like I'm torturing you when I change your diaper

gave me no choice but to take away your board books for fear you would choke on the chunks you've been

eating out of them

still get up in the middle of the night to eat

crawl underneath chairs, get stuck, and scream

won't wear socks, and sneer at me when I threaten to tape them to your legs when it's snowing

figured out a way to take off your new ankle zip boots within 13 minutes of wearing them

don't like avocados

like prunes

I wouldn't trade you for the world. That smile... those hugs... you've got me.

Love, Mama

Don't tell anybody, but I was the kid in high school who collected three or four different pens the night before my semester-long English journal was due so I could write my entries all at once—but still have them look like they were entered at different times. It's not that I didn't enjoy writing, exactly, it's that I was incapable of the self-discipline required to maintain a journal. Even so, I continued to amass an enormous collection of Really Cool Blank Books (RCBB) only to have them sit around looking cool, but sadly empty. It wasn't until I discovered the world of blogging that I started writing on a regular basis. When I first started my blog (titled "a swoop and a dart," from an e.e. cummings poem), I thought I would eventually turn most of my entries into scrapbook pages. Now I realize that my blog doesn't have to be anything other than what it already is: an anthology of my life, written by me, with an occasional picture thrown in for illustrative purposes to share with family and friends. Do I still turn entries into scrapbook pages? Yes. Do I feel compelled to do that with each one? Absolutely not. My writing is valuable enough as is.

DATE

No\vember 23, 1936

EVENT

Life Magazine Debut

12 x 12 photo book
by Anna Aspnes

LIFE MAGAZINE WAS CREATED IN 1936 BY TIME founder Henry Luce, and it soon became wildly popular. The magazine assigned as much importance to photos as it did to words, which was uncommon for a magazine at that time. As a result, *Life* became very influential.

Inspired by the trademark photojournalism found in years of *Life* magazine, Anna tackled a monumental project: with as much photographic detail as possible, capture a day in the life of her family. A total of 198 photos found their way into her digital photobook, providing a very complete snapshot of the Aspnes household. To organize so many images, Anna gathered and edited them first and placed them in a single location on her computer. She then created a sub-folder for each double-page spread. To complete her design, she chose a simple digital stamp to add a subtle embellishment to her pages and formatted her text into magazine-style columns.

Family Time

One of the reasons we go through this rigmarole every weekend, and on holidays too for that matter, is that it gives us the opportunity to spend quality time as a family.

I was raised that way. Eric was raised that way. I remember as a teen, that my parents, sister and I were so busy with our own lives that it was the one time of day that we actually got to sit down together.

As Ella and Luke get older they too will begin to form lives of their own that will include friends, sports and hobbies that lead them on their own paths. If we can instill this concept in them now then I am hoping we will always have that opportunity to talk and eat together and remain close as a family unit. That is my intention.

Needless to say, living the moment isn't quite so hunky dory as it sounds and meal times rarely pass without some sort of drama. It's just a fact of life with small children.

Challenge number one has always been keeping Luke interested in his food long enough to keep him at the table for more than 5 minutes. There was a time we couldn't walk into a restaurant because Luke was such a nightmare in this department. I remember having to order our meals to go one time because all he wanted to do was run around between the tables and by not

allowing him to do that, he chose to scream at the top of his lungs.

Oddly enough on this day, Ella was the problem. I once knew a girl who told me that "4 year olds are like 2 years on crack". Ella's pretty laidback so I wouldn't go that far, however, she's definitely shaping up to be a Drama Queen. First comes the pout and now we're starting to venture into the "storming off" stage. Eric thinks she's a nightmare now but he's got no idea. I've warned him that the teen years are going to make now look like a teddy bear's picnic.

This particular pout was all over the fork and spoon she was using. She's very particular about her "silverware". She usually has the Disney Princesses or Care Bear while Luke generally gets Sponge Bob or the frog ones from that I got him from the Rainforest Cafe. On this particular day, she wanted the frogs. Totally bizarre but then she is a woman and you know what they say about a woman's prerogative.

To cut a convoluted story short, Luke teased her a little (and of course true to his personality enjoyed every minute of it), before deciding to offer her his frog fork, by which time she didn't want it. Typical! She was over it and moving on, we proceeded to enjoy breakfast with Luke obsessing over his "bleeding" barely-existing boo-boo and usual table antics.

Family Time

One of the reasons we go through this rigmarole every weekend, and on holidays too for that matter, is that it gives us the opportunity to spend quality time as a family.

I was raised that way. Eric was raised that way. I remember as a teen, that my parents, sister and I were so busy with our own lives that it was the one time of day that we actually got to sit down together.

As Ella and Luke get older they too will begin to form lives of their own that will include friends, sports and hobbies that lead them on their own paths. If we can instill this concept in them now then I am hoping we will always have that opportunity to talk and eat together and remain close as a family unit. That is my intention.

Needless to say, living the moment isn't quite so hunky dory as it sounds and meal times rarely pass without some sort of drama. It's just a fact of life with small children.

Challenge number one has always been keeping Luke interested in his food long enough to keep him at the table for more than 5 minutes. There was a time we couldn't walk into a restaurant because Luke was such a nightmare in this department. I remember having to order our meals to go one time because all he wanted to do was run around between the tables and by not

allowing him to do that, he chose to scream at the top of his lungs.

Oddly enough on this day, Ella was the problem. I once knew a girl who told me that "4 year olds are like 2 years on crack". Ella's pretty laidback so I wouldn't go that far however, she's definitely shaping up to be a Drama Queen. First comes the pout and now we're starting to venture into the "storming off" stage. Eric thinks she's a nightmare now but he's got no idea. I've warned him that the teen years are going to make now look like a teddy bear's picnic.

This particular pout was all over the fork and spoon she was using. She's very particular about her "silverware". She usually has the Disney Princesses or Care Bear while Luke generally gets Sponge Bob or the frog ones from that I got him from the Rainforest Cafe. On this particular day, she wanted the frogs. Totally bizarre but then she is a woman and you know what they say about a woman's prerogative.

To cut a convoluted story short, Luke teased her a little (and of course true to his personality enjoyed every minute of it), before deciding to offer her his frog fork, by which time she didn't want it. Typical! She was over it and moving on, we proceeded to enjoy breakfast with Luke obsessing over his 'bleeding' barely-existing boo-boo and usual table antics.

10

11

Out and About

So it's already 1:30pm and we're just heading out. Where did the time go? And we didn't even have dance class today.

Ella usually has dance for about 45 minutes at 12:30pm every Saturday but with Summer fast approaching and busy weekends she hasn't been for a few weeks. Summers in Alaska are always like that so we've made the decision to take a break until the Fall.

It is always madness getting everyone and everything in into the car, making sure we have juice, snacks, diapers, shopping list, my purse, my camera, my ID etc. It's not all that unusual for me to forget something, especially with Eric rushing me out the door.

The car wash is the first on the list. We're really bad with getting the car into the car wash but there doesn't seem much point when it turns around and snows or rains right after. Ella loves the car wash. She thinks it's a blast but Luke has his reservations, peeking out from behind his hands. He is deathly afraid of any loud rumbling noises. Meanwhile Eric polishes up the inside of the car throwing a duster at me while he's at it.

We talk about grabbing a Starbucks but Eric forgets and ends up flipping a U-turn. He goes through the drive through. I don't. I like to walk in. Hard to believe we'll spend $6.20 on two coffees, but we do. Every time. I've never drank coffee, not even through college but with 2 children, a house to keep and a

business to run I find I need the boost at about 2-4pm to get me through the rest of the day. It's quite fortuitous that our good friend Melissa is working the window. Ella of course is highly confused and we spend the next 5 mins trying to explain the ins and outs of having to work to no avail.

With a tall skinny latte in hand we head for Costcos. On average we make this trip bi-weekly, mainly because we can't seem to step into the place without spending a couple of hundred dollars.

I end up ridiculing Eric for his penchant of having to park right next to the door and he in turn gives me a hard time for not holding Ella's hand while walking into the store. This constant banter may be bizarre but it makes our marriage work.

Ella and Luke like Costcos. There are wide aisles to run in, places to hide and an endless supply of food samples.

16

Winding Down

Daddy does the dishes, Mommy tidies up the rest of the house and then we begin to wind down for the evening.

This includes time with the children, or if they are doing their own thing, some computer time for us. Eric catches up with on-line college classes and attack my inbox.

On this day we had just received Chocolate eggs from Mama and Papa. Ella took it upon herself to start taking them out of the box when Luke caught on and wanted in on the action. Sharing is not always their strong point. I managed to diffuse the spat calmly and they ended up sharing the Maltesers. We love English chocolate and it's always a bit special when you get some at Easter.

Ella and Luke grow in spurts and both wake up in the night literally screaming. Ella's knees and Luke's feet are hotspots. During these times we use old faithful Motrin in order to ensure a restful night for all.

Bed time is a team effort. Ella and Luke are both tired so it can be the most difficult part of the day. Ella brushes her teeth with a follow-up by me. Luke, on the other hand, hates having his teeth brushed. Until recently we had to literally pin him down until he reluctantly accepted the fact that this was going to happen every day, twice per day, no matter what.

Getting them actually into their own beds is also a challenge. Luke loves to annoy Ella by getting into her bed and they always get distracted.

By the time I climb into bed with Ella to read my eyes are burning and I'm ready to crash. But, I love that story/chatting time one on one with her. This is when we do our Mommy/Daughter bonding.

When both are officially asleep there is a huge sense of relief. The house is at last still and it's at this point that I should probably go to bed myself as Eric does. After all, I will have to start all over again in less than 12 hours. But, as much as my body desires the sleep, this time has become my time and I enjoy having the entire house to myself. While I love my family and my children, I relish the time on my own equally as much.

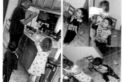

20

21

"this moment contains all ♥ moments."
—c.s. lewis

8½ x 11 page
by Mi'Chelle Larsen

BOUNDLESS INSPIRATION can be found in the life and works of great authors and thinkers. Such is the case with Irish writer C.S. Lewis, author of scores of philosophical works as well as the famous children's series, *The Chronicles of Narnia*. Lewis's insight into the human condition makes him an inspirational resource for layouts about family, love, faith, and the meaning of life.

Mi'Chelle's layout is a perfect match for this C.S. Lewis quote. When she first found this photo, she cried. For her, it speaks volumes about what happiness as a mother is all about, and without a doubt she knew that the photo should take precedence over all else on the page. She purposely chose not to include journaling, relying on the simple quote to beautifully and succinctly express the emotion of the image.

DATE
Late November

EVENT
Ohio State vs. Michigan
Football Game

8½ x 11 page

OSU girl

I did not go to Ohio State, despite my family's many connections to Columbus. Instead, I went to Miami University a few hours southwest while I never once regretted that decision, I have wished on occasion that I could have gone to both. Luckily, if you grow up an Ohio State girl, they let you remain an Ohio State girl. Because Daddy was in the marching band in the '60s, I have wonderful childhood memories of alumni band weekends, skull sessions, and being the lucky recipient of the 2nd season ticket to attend football games. I was raised with a healthy disdain for Michigan in general and the University of Michigan in particular, and was telling my first Michigan joke—directions to Ann Arbor—around age 3. I still grow teary hearing Across the field or watching Script Ohio appear. Life screeches to a halt each chilly November for the most important game of the year. Ohio State vs. Michigan. No other game matters quite as much. I'm a Buckeye at heart.

Across the Field

Fight the team across the field
Show them Ohio's here
(We've got the team why don't we)
Set the Earth reverberating
With a mighty cheer
RAH! RAH! RAH!
Hit them hard and see how they fall!
Never let that team get the ball
Hail! Hail! The gang's all here
So let's win that old conference now!

—OSU's fight song, the oldest college
fight song still in current use (written in 1915)

THE OHIO STATE UNIVERSITY VS. University of Michigan rivalry began in 1897, and since that time it has sparked one of the most famous annual football matchups in the country. Rivalries make sports more intense, and every level of competition (and every sport, for that matter) has one. It's enough to turn a normally mild-mannered mama into a sewing-machine-wielding sports fanatic who whips up adorable clothing with the home team's name all over it for her four-year-old.

This photo of me at four has always been one of my favorite childhood snapshots. I loved going to Ohio State football games as a kid, and I wanted my layout to capture the excitement I felt—and still feel today—when it comes time to play Michigan in the final game. If you have a favorite team in a favorite sport, you understand how electrifying a long-standing rivalry can be. Why not create a page about it this season? If the traditions and drama surrounding sporting events are as important in your house as they are in mine, they deserve mention in your scrapbooks. Go team!

8½ x 11 page
by Laura Kurz

We recently came across this photo of my great uncle Frankie, sometime in his twenties (during the 1930s). The resemblance from him to cousin Ryan (right side at his high school graduation in 2005) is almost unbelievable.

resemblance

date: 3105/05

Frankie was Ryan's great uncle as well (he was our grandmother Mary's brother). We never met our great uncle Frankie, he passed away suddenly in his forties, but I'm sure he would have loved to see the resemblance in his great nephew.

family

TIP: *The Alliance for Children and Families encourages everyone to participate in activities that play a role in strengthening families, from planning a shared meal with your children's classmates and their families to volunteering as a family to improve your community. This year, why not take an active role in National Family Week? You can request additional information and a planning kit to help plan your event directly from the organization at their website, alliance1.org.*

THE ALLIANCE FOR Children and Families has sponsored National Family Week for over 30 years, working tirelessly to advance the idea that family connections are the building blocks of strong families, and that strong families translate into strong communities.

As a scrapbooker, you know that family connections can be found anywhere and everywhere, and even the smallest connection is capable of conveying great love. Family resemblance is one such connection. Laura and her family were amazed to discover the strong physical resemblance between her cousin Ryan and her great-uncle Frankie, two blood relatives who never had the chance to meet. It's a special feeling to know you have a connection with an ancestor— whether physical or personality-driven—and it fosters a sense of belonging in a family. What family connections can you scrapbook about this month?

DATE

Late November

EVENT

World Hello Day

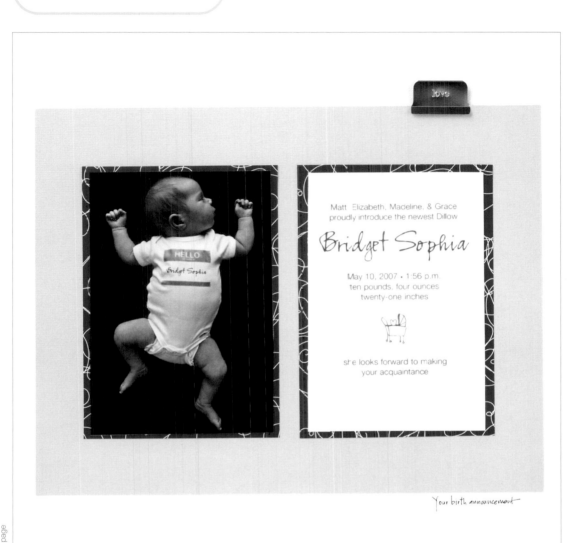

12 x 12 page

Your birth announcement

WORLD HELLO DAY IS A LITTLE-KNOWN CELEBRATION created in 1973 as a response to the Arab-Israeli conflict. The goal is to encourage each person to greet ten others in the name of peace.

The first time I heard of World Hello Day I immediately thought of the nametag stickers given out at school functions and office meetings that say "Hello My Name Is." After Bridget was born, it occurred to me that this would be a clever way to announce a baby's birth—after all, what is more peace-filled than saying hello to a newborn baby? My World Hello Day-inspired birth announcements were easy to make—and easy to turn into a scrapbook layout. The whole project took very little time to create, making it a perfect fit for a new mother.

4 x 6 card

Tip: *Thanks to the magic of heat transfer material, just about anything you can print from your home printer can be ironed on to the fabric of your choice.*

153

December

1
2
3
4
5
6
7
8
9
10
11
12
This month... 13
bake cookies, preserve recipes 14
snap a photo every day 15
find comfort at home 16
discover metaphors in puzzling places 17
shop, shop, shop (and rock) 18
celebrate the magic of chocolate 19
skip the "will-do" list and make a "have-done" list 20
21
22
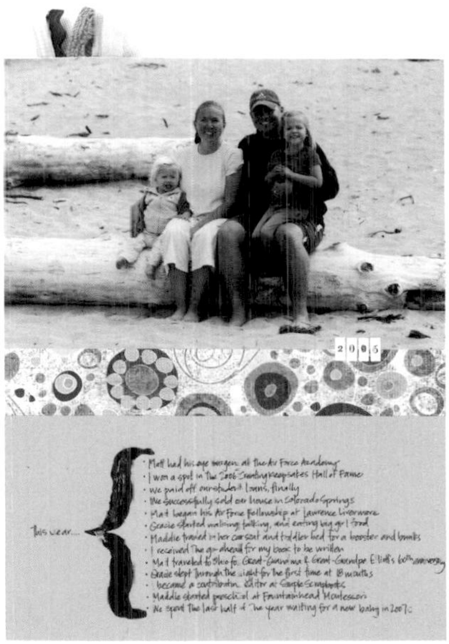

23
24
25
26
27
28
29
30
31

THE COOKIE CUTTER COLLECTORS CLUB IS A small organization—650 members strong—with a big passion for humble cookie cutters, the tinsmiths who create them, and the art and memories associated with baking cut-out cookies.

TIP: *It's easier than you think to make custom scalloped edges. Take the corner guide (the thing that lines the paper up in the right position) off a corner rounder and start punching! Practice makes perfect, says Mi'Chelle; there is a definite learning curve to master lining up the edges properly. Once all the scallops are punched, use a small hole punch to make the hole in each of the scallops. Careful, this is addicting—Mi'Chelle reports the presence of a lot of scallops on random papers in her house.*

Mi'Chelle created this double-duty mini-album, both a useful cookie cookbook and a cute piece of kitchen décor, as a gift for a bridal shower. She formatted the recipes into circles using a circle guide in Photoshop, printed and adhered them to beautiful patterned paper, and hooked them all together on a jump ring with a few cookie cutters attached for the bride-to-be. Cookbooks are a great shower or wedding gift, and handmade collections like this are sure to be loved and passed on to future generations of cookie-bakers!

cinnamon cookies

1 c. sugar
1/2 c. butter, softened
3 egg yolks
2 T. milk

2 c. flour
2 t. cinnamon
1/2 t. baking powder
1/2 t. salt

Cream butter and sugar. Beat in egg yolks, then stir in milk. Sift dry ingredients together, then add to wet ingredients until well blended. Chill for 2 hours. Roll dough 1/4" thick, cut, bake at 350 degrees for 10-12 minutes, until lightly browned Remove cookies to a wire rack to cool.

gourmet sugar cookies

cream:
2 c. butter
1 1/2 c. sugar

add:
4 egg yolks
2 t. vanilla
4 1/2 c. flour
1/2 t. salt

Knead 7 or 8 times, adding flour as needed to make a non sticky dough.
Chill for 1 hour.
Roll dough 1/4" thick

Bake at 350 F for 8-10 minutes until barely golden around edges.

handmade a bum
by Mi'Chelle Larsen

THERE'S A GOOD CHANCE THAT DECEMBER 14 is just another day in your house, but in our house, it's a big day: our Gracie's birthday. Pencil this universal birthday project idea into the appropriate square of your calendar and then go ahead and have a piece of cake today to celebrate in advance!

I take a lot of pictures. Thousands of pictures, actually—when you start young you've got a lot of time to amass a collection! What I don't do usually, however, is take pictures every single day. That's why I love photo-a-day challenges. I was first introduced to the concept over at *twopeasinabucket.com* a

Dear Gracie,

Happy Birthday, sweet girl!

Inside this little book you'll find 31 photos that help to tell the story of what you were like the month you turned two years old, should you ever be inclined to wonder. It isn't a complete story, but it is 100% your story. Life with you is never, ever boring, that's for sure.

We hope you always know how much we love and adore you.

Love,
Mama and Da
December 2006

music class

Music Together has been quite an experience. A few months ago, when you started your first formal activity, I was certain that we would last a week, maybe two. It didn't seem to be your thing, all that following-instructions-and-singing-and-dancing-and-being-smiled-at-by-the-friendly-teacher-stuff. It took a while before you were willing to play along just a little, still turning into Mary Jane Sticky Baby for no apparent reason. I'm happy to report, however, that somewhere along the way you started to really enjoy it, and even smile back once in a while.

few years ago. The discipline required to see a whole month through was exhausting, but it was also one of the most creatively inspiring challenges I've ever tried. For this project, I decided to narrow the scope even further and take a photo each day of the month that Gracie turned two, focusing solely on her activities and personality. I'm already wildly attached to this album, because she changes so fast. It isn't feasible for me to put together an album like this for each of my children every year, but it is definitely a project I'll do again in the future.

6 x 12 album

...IITC. blaze with the firethat is nevere r beautieS which I try to catch as they anyone who keeps theability to seebeau so sweet.Emily Dickinson gonna get-Forrest.Gump

December 27

aunt katherine

Your Aunt Katherine adores you, and you adore her. You've never been able to say Katherine until this visit, when you started saying "Kaffren" with authority. You first met your Aunt Katherine at two weeks of age, when your favorite activity was to sit on her lap and sleep while she knitted. At two years, you prefer to play more active games, chasing each other wildly in the backyard and joining in the old classic, "Wildebeest." She understands you in a very special way, and you are lucky to have her in your life.

t youre Bestrong, go with your h .Loveas though you havenever been h of intelligent people and theaffection thers, to leave the world a bit better, w

December 31

a snapshot of you

You're two.
You have the happiest, most genuine smile.
You are opinionated.
Things need to be your idea.
You love your sister unconditionally.
You love your parents unconditionally.
You don't so much love the cat unconditionally.
Your vocabulary has exploded in the last month.
You take one nap a day, usually from 1:00-2:40 pm.
You wake up each morning between 6:30-6:50 am.
You go to bed each night between 7:00-7:30 pm.
You are so excited to become a big sister in 2007.
We are so excited to watch you grow every day.

5 x 7 accordion album
by Mi'Chelle Larsen

AUTHOR JANE AUSTEN WROTE PRIMARILY about life inside the home: customs, manners, relationships, and the lives of women. Her novels were published anonymously—it was only within the safe confines of her own home and with her family that she shared her writings freely.

Inspired by a quote from Austen's novel *Emma,* ("Ah, there is nothing like staying home for real comfort.") Mi'Chelle knew it was time to come clean and document her inner homebody—the one who would choose to hang out in a calm, comfortable environment over doing just about anything else. Using simple photos of places in her home that give her the strongest sense of tranquility and reflect her desire for calm, Mi'Chelle provides a window into her personality. She's someone who, if given the chance, would really enjoy sitting down with Jane Austen for a chat.

It has long been evident to me that I am a homebody. I used to try to be one of those interesting people who loved being out on the town. but it never felt right. Fortunately I've learned to embrace my inner-hobbit and simply celebrate the comforts of the place I call home.

"Ah! there is nothing like staying at home for real comfort." --Jane Austen

i love being surrounded by pictures -- evidence of life

i love having space to create + admire beautiful things.

i love curling up on the sofa with a good book or a baby or a nice warm husband

12 x 12 page

DID YOU KNOW THE CROSSWORD puzzle is the most popular word game in the world? It first appeared in a Sunday newspaper (the *New York World*) in 1913. Before long, the crossword spread like wildfire and could be found in almost every newspaper in the country.

I leave most of the crossword puzzling to my Ma because, for someone who loves words as much as I do, I'm frighteningly bad at crossword puzzles. But I was thinking one day about these puzzles, and how they're not unlike life with the average spunky 2-year-old (e.g., Miss Gracie Dillow). Crosswords and toddlers both get progressively harder as the week goes on, often stretching you beyond your wits' end, but they also inspire lots of smiles and satisfaction along the way. Do you know anyone who reminds you of a crossword puzzle (or game)? Explore the comparison on a layout!

DATE

December 26

EVENT

Boxing Day

12 x 12 page
by Mary MacAskill

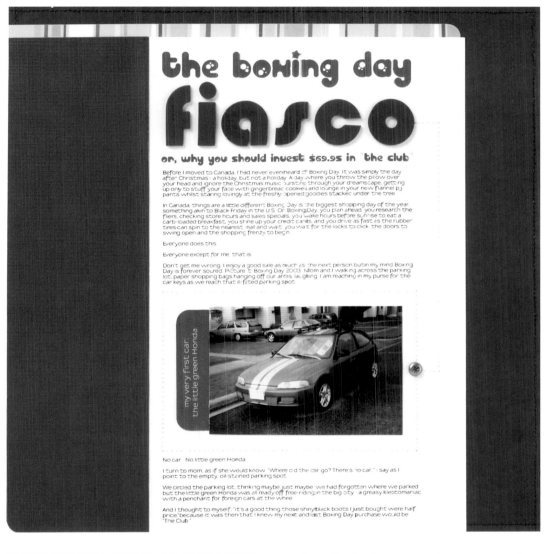

THINK BOXING DAY IS AN OCCASION to drag all the empty packaging from newly exchanged Christmas gifts out to the curb? Think again. Boxing Day originated in Great Britain, supposedly from the practice of rich lords giving gifts to their servants after Christmas. The gifts were "boxed up," and the servants were given the day off to celebrate.

Today, Boxing Day celebrations typically center around shopping. Such is the case with Mary, whose Boxing Day power-shopping excursion ended in frustration one year after she discovered her car had been stolen. Remember: it's OK to journal about the "other side" of a holiday—not all celebrations go according to plan, and not all scrapbook pages need to present a perfect picture of each minute of a holiday get-together. It's enough to tell a simple story and make it available to the people you love.

12 x 12 page
by Mary MacAskill

HOW FITTING IN A HOLIDAY SEASON full of hustle and bustle that there should be a day dedicated to one of life's great pleasures: chocolate. (I don't know about you, but I can think of 364 other days in the year that would be improved by a little chocolate celebration, too!) We have the National Confectioners Association to thank for National Chocolate Day, the official day to honor America's favorite flavor.

Do you have a favorite chocolate treat? Mary does, and she documented her love for (and powerlessness in the face of) Twix with clever "stop-action" photography of the disappearing candy bar. Her journaling is more than a documentation of her favorite temptation—it's also a window into her witty personality and writing style. See? Chocolate is good for you in so many ways.

DATE

December 31

EVENT

New Year's Eve

I'M NOT REALLY A FAN of New Year's Resolutions because I'm just no good at them. I always start out strong doing whatever superhuman feat I've declared I will accomplish. But, as February rolls around, there is definite evidence that I'm regressing to my slacker ways. It's not good for my year's outlook to be fighting a losing battle so soon.

This year, I say "enough." Don't make a list of what you want to accomplish in the year ahead. Instead, take a little time on New Year's Eve to make a list of what you accomplished last year. Your list will serve as a positive reminder that you really do get a lot done! Gussy up your list with some pretty paper and a photo of yourself or your family, and you've got a quick year-in-review scrapbook page you can be proud of.

8½ x 11 page

2006

This year....

{
- Matt had his eye surgery at the Air Force Academy
- I won a spot in The 2006 Creating Keepsakes Hall of Fame
- We paid off our student loans, finally
- We successfully sold our house in Colorado Springs
- Matt began his Air Force Fellowship at Lawrence Livermore
- Gracie started walking, talking, and eating big girl food
- Maddie traded in her car seat and toddler bed for a booster and bunks
- I received the go-ahead for my book to be written
- Matt traveled to Ohio for Great-Grandma & Great-Grandpa Elliott's 60th anniversary
- Gracie slept through the night for the first time at 18 months
- I became a contributing editor at Simple Scrapbooks
- Maddie started preschool at Fountainhead Montessori
- We spent the last half of the year waiting for a new baby in 2007!
}

TIP: *Make your embellishments work harder! Try choosing items that not only coordinate with your favorite paper but also support your message. Case in point: see the five ribbons at the top of the page? I loved how the products from two different companies coordinated so nicely, but I also love how those five ribbons symbolize my family— four pink ones for the girls, one blue one for the boy. Only see three girls in this photo? We did too, until we realized later that this was the first photo taken of our family as a family of five, because I was pregnant and just didn't know it yet.*

Resources

January

12. THE CREATIVITY BOOK
creativelyspeakinig.com/creativity_month.html
materials handmade album • patterned paper (Danny O for K & Company, Li'l Davis Designs) • chipboard book label (Maya Road) • paint (Delta) • rubber stamp (Paper Source) • rub-ons (American Crafts, Scrapworks) • book rings (Staples) • miscellaneous ephemera • AL Modern Type font • *7 x 5 flip album by Elizabeth Dillow, Arlington, VA*

14. LIFE AND TIMES
materials 3-ring binder album (Maya Road) • calendar (Creative Imaginations) • patterned paper (Daisy D's, Anna Griffin, KI Memories, Karen Foster) • rub-ons (My Mind's Eye, American Crafts, Scrapworks) • font (Sandra Oh) • *4½ x 8½ binder and embellished calendar by Mi'Chelle Larsen, Bountiful, UT*

15. THE FLOWER CROWN
tournamentofroses.com
materials paper flowers (Prima) • rub-ons (American Crafts) • *8½ x 11 page by Elizabeth Dillow, Arlington, VA*

16. MY FAMILY
materials album (7Gypsies) • rub-ons (American Crafts) • scroll stamp (Fontwerks) • paint (Making Memories) • Splendid 66 font • *6½ x 3 mini-album by Laura Kurz, Baltimore, MD*

18. NEW YEAR'S DAY pg. 18
materials patterned paper (Making Memories, Scenic Route, Colorbök, Basic Grey) • letter stickers (Basic Grey) • diecut (Scribble Scrabble) • foam adhesive (All Night Media) • corner rounder (Creative Memories) • font (Caecilia Roman) • *8½ x 11 page by Margaret Scarbrough, Butte Valley, CA*

19. CLEARLY, IT WAS NOT HER BEST YEAR
materials patterned paper (Scenic Route) • rub-ons (7Gypsies) • chipboard star (Heidi Swapp) • font (AL Modern Type) • *12 x 12 page by Elizabeth Dillow, Arlington, VA*

20. DINOSAURS
materials metal tin (Teresa Collins for Junkitz) • patterned paper (Stemma) • chipboard letters and frame (Li'l Davis Designs) • transparency (3M) • eyelets (Making Memories) • corner rounder (Creative Memories) • staples • Zupagargonizer, Gill Sans, Gill Sans Light, Dakota, Book Antiqua fonts • *7½ x 5½ tin by Margaret Scarbrough, Butte Valley, CA*

21. HAPPY WEDNESDAY, FRIEND
friendshipandgoodwill.org/observances.html
materials metal lunchbox (Basic Grey) • patterned paper (Scenic Route) • rub-ons (7 Gypsies, American Crafts) • rubber stamps (Fontwerks, 7Gypsies) • felt flowers (American Crafts) • jeweled brads (Making Memories) • chain (Making Memories) • calendar (Graphique de France) • greeting card (Koco New York) • *lunchbox project by Elizabeth Dillow, Arlington, VA*

22. HANDWRITTEN
materials album (Maple Lane Press by EK Success) • patterned paper (SEI) • rub-ons (American Crafts) • tag (Making Memories) • *11 x 8½ album by Elizabeth Dillow, Arlington, VA*

February

26. DEVINE RECIPES
materials mini-album (Making Memories) • rub-ons (7Gypsies) • alphabet stickers (American Crafts) • ribbon (Strano Designs) • transparencies (My Mine's Eye) • silver tabs (KI Memories) • Splendid 66 font • *4 x 4 mini-album by Laura Kurz, Baltimore, MD*

28. 274
materials patterned paper, heart die cut, rub-ons (Heidi Grace Designs) • rubber stamps, jump ring (Making Memories) • foam adhesive (All Night Media) • *12 x 12 page by Elizabeth Dillow, Arlington, VA*

29. TEN
womenssportsfoundation.org
materials rub-ons (Hambly Screen Prints, Making Memories) • gaffer tape (7Gypsies) • photo turns, brads (Making Memories) • paint (Delta) • AL Modern Type font • *12 x 12 page by Elizabeth Dillow, Arlington, VA*

30. DAYS TO RELIVE
materials chipboard covers (7Gypsies) • patterned paper (American Crafts, Scenic Route) • map (Rand McNally) • staff paper (Passantino) • rubber stamp (Fontwerks) • paint (Delta) • rub-ons (Creative Imaginations) • gaffer tape (7Gypsies) • tab punch (McGill) • book rings (Staples) • AL Modern Type, Hoefler Text fonts • *5 x 5 handmade album by Elizabeth Dillow, Arlington, VA*

32. 12
materials 12 x 12 album (Bazzill Basics Paper) • patterned paper (MOD for Autumn Leaves, MAMBI, K & Company, Adornit Carolee's Creations, Rusty Pickle, KI Memories, Creative Imaginations) • chipboard numbers (Basic Grey) • slide mounts (Jest Charming) • *12 x 12 album by Elizabeth Dillow, Arlington, VA*

34. UNDERSTANDING ANNAREXIA
digital materials photo book (www.shutterfly.com) • digital papers (Timeworn #1 by by Dana Zarling (www.designerdigitals.com), Black Eyed Pea Page Set by Rhonna Farrer (www.twopeasinabucket.com), Science Matters Page Set by Jennifer Adams Donnelly (www.designerdigitals.com), Book Bag Essentials by Gina Cabrera (www.digitaldesignessentials.com), Altered Pattern Paper # 4 and #6 by Jackie Eckles (www.designerdigitals.com) • Brush Sets/Digital Stamp Sets: (Boho Flourish and Corner Flourish Brush Sets by Michelle Coleman (www.scrapartist.com), Ledger, Ticked No. 2, Brushes by Katie Pertiet, Stamped Statements (www.designerdigitals.com), Science Matters Page Set by Jennifer Adams Donnelly (www.designerdigitals.com), Corner It Brush Set by Jackie Eckles (www.designerdigitals.com), Artistique & Magnificent Page Sets, Labeled Number, Labeled Female, Scanty Journal Lines, Floral Silhouette Brush Sets by Anna Aspnes (www.designerdigitals.com), Book Bag Essentials by Gina Cabrera (www.digitaldesignessentials.com) • digital elements (Fanciful Embellies by Jackie Eckles, Free Spirit by Maya (www.scrapbookgraphics.com), StudioGirls Basics Collection Grungy Polaroid and Filmstrip by Maya, Zipstrip on Canvas by Jennifer Bolton, (www.scrapbookgraphics.com)) • stock photos (www.sxc.hu) • P22 Cezanne, Uptown, Fluoxetine, Klill-LightTailX, Impact, Fountain Pen Frenzy fonts • *8 x 8 photo book by Anna Aspnes, Elmendorf AFB, AK*

36. CHINESE NEW YEAR
materials board book (www.augresources.com) • patterned paper (Basic Grey) • brush sets/digital stamp sets (Ledger Super Pack Brushes by Katie Pertiet, Stamped Statements (www.designerdigitals.com), Buddhist Way Brushes by Maya (www.scrapbookgraphics.com)) • miscellaneous found items • Klill LightTailX, Fountain Pen Frenzy fonts • *5 x 5 mini-album by Anna Aspnes, Elmendorf AFB, AK*

37. BUILD ON FAILURE
materials alphabet sticker (Heidi Swapp) • bird transparency (My Mind's Eye) • Print Clearly font • *11 x 8½ page by Laura Kurz, Baltimore, MD*

March

40. CIRCA 34
materials chipboard album (Zsiage) • patterned paper (Adornit Carolee's Creations, Sweetwater, Around the Block, Basic Grey, Provo Craft) • fabric stickers (SEI) • chipboard numbers (American Crafts) • paper flower (Making Memories) • tag (My Mind's Eye) • book rings (Staples) • *8 x 4 handmade album by Elizabeth Dillow, Arlington, VA*

42. ART FRIDAY
acminet.org/youth_art_month.htm
materials corkboard squares • chipboard letters (Li'l Davis Designs) • paint (Delta) • acrylic stamp (Adornit Carolee's Creations) • rubber stamp (Paper Source) • ribbon (Stemma) • silver tab, bead chain (Making Memories) • pop dot • bulldog clips • (not sure how to word a home décor project) • *12 x 20 wall hanging by Elizabeth Dillow, Arlington, VA*

43. TRACES OF LOVE
materials fabric (Moda, others unknown) • rub-ons (American Crafts) • corner rounder (EK Success) • Crop-A-Dile (We R Memory Keepers) • note: Mi'Chelle used the corner rounder and Crop-A-Dile to make the lacy scallop • *8½ x 11 page by Mi'Chelle Larsen, Bountiful, UT*

44. WHAT'S YOUR NAME?
materials album (Trace Industries) • patterned paper (Tinkering Ink) • transparency overlays (My Mind's Eye) • rub-ons (Making Memories, Scrapworks) • ink (Clearsnap) • paint (Ranger Inks) • *4 x 6 mini-album by Mi'Chelle Larsen, Bountiful, UT*

46. ANY GIVEN WEDNESDAY
digital materials Photoshop Elements 3.0 (www.adobesystems.com) • brushes (www.photoshopbrushes.com) • Steelfish font • *12 x 12 page by Mary MacAskill, Calgary, AB*

47. GIRL SCOUT HISTORY
materials box (Rackel Industries) • patterned paper, rub-ons, stickers (K & Company) • fabric numbers (Girl Scouts of the United States of America) • ribbon • *8 x 10 covered keepsake box by Elizabeth Dillow, Arlington, VA*

48. IS SHE BANANNAS?
digital materials Photoshop CS2 (Adobe Systems) • photobook (Shutterfly) • patterned papers (Altered Pattern Paper #1, 4 and 6, Ledger Paper from Take Notes Page Set by Jackie Eckles (www.designerdigitals.com), All Mapped Out by Katie Pertiet (www.designerdigitals.com), Kraft Card and Graph Paper from Book Bag Essentials by Gina Cabrera (www.digitaldesignessentials.com) • brushes and digital stamps (Ledger Super Pack, Touch Up Paint, Between the Lines Journal Brush Sets by Katie Pertiet (www.designerdigitals.com), Clippings Quote, Highlight, Painted Dribbles Brush Sets by Jackie Eckles (www.designerdigitals.com), Painted Circle Splatz, Summer SoNo, Spring Doodles Brush Sets by Anna Aspnes (www.designerdigitals.com), Buddhist Way Brush Set by Maya (www.scrapbookgraphics.com)) • elements (Altered Embellies: Hats, Flowers 2, Arrows 1 and Circles 2, Altered Overlays 1, Stars from Market Page Set, Doodle It Variety 2, 20 Oct 2006 Designer Digital Web Challenge Freebie, 24 Dec 2006 Designer Digitals Ad Challenge Freebie by Jackie Eckles (www.designerdigitals.com), Ledger Chipboard Alpha by Katie Pertiet (www.designerdigitals.com), Quirky Good Vibes and Existence Quotes and Boxes, and Maya Doll Templates by Maya (www.scrapbookgraphics.com), Simple Torn Edges, Naked Tape It and Naked Tape It Freestyle Elements, Stitching and Staples (recolored) from Sk8ter Dude Page Set by Anna Aspnes (www.designerdigitals.com), shoe and brain brushes from Anna's personal collection • Fountain Pen Frenzy, 4990810, Diomedez, OK Good Day, Times New Roman, Rock It, 1942 Report, Wazoo, Wiffles fonts • *8 x 8 photo book by Anna Aspnes, Elmendorf AFB, AK*

50. MARCH MADNESS 2007
materials album kit (EK Success) • patterned paper (Scenic Route) • rub-ons (Scrapworks) • *4 x 7¾ spiral album by Elizabeth Dillow, Arlington, VA*

51. INCREDIBLY HAPPY
campfireusa.org
materials patterned paper (Karen Russell for Creative Imaginations) • acrylic stamp (Autumn Leaves) • ribbon, brads, jump ring, paint (Making Memories) • plastic flowers (Heidi Grace Designs) • charm • *12 x 12 page by Elizabeth Dillow, Arlington, VA*

54. POETRY THAT MATTERS
materials album (Maple Lane Press by EK Success) • patterned paper (Making Memories, Around the Block, Stampin' Up, Basic Grey, Flair Designs, Chatterbox, Rusty Pickle, Creative Imaginations, Danny O for K & Company, Cosmo Cricket) • flower transparency (My Mind's Eye) • acrylic stamp (Adornit Carolee's Creations) • rubber stamp (7 Gypsies) • chipboard letter stickers (American Crafts) • metal ribbon charm (Making Memories) • ribbon • AL Modern Type and Baskerville fonts • *11 x 8½ album by Elizabeth Dillow, Arlington, VA*

56. MY NAME IS PAUL
materials board book (Westrim Crafts) • patterned paper (Scenic Route) • rub-ons (Stemma, Scrapworks) • small puzzle piece (Inkadinkado) • large puzzle pieces (Creative Imaginations) • Abadi MT Condensed Extra Bold font • photos by Linda and Judd Serotta • *6½ x 6½ mini-album by Elizabeth Dillow, Arlington, VA*

58. LEARNING TO FLY
nationalkitemonth.org
materials patterned paper, letter stickers (American Crafts) • text embellishments (K Memories) • corner rounder (Creative Memories) • clear index tab • Gill Sans font • *11 x 8½ page by Margaret Scarbrough, Butte Valley, CA*

59. ON BEING A CLEVELAND INDIANS FAN
materials patterned paper (Scenic Route) • label sticker (7Gypsies) • chipboard letter (Basic Grey) • paint (Delta) • chipboard bracket (Fancy Pants Designs) • *12 x 12 page by Elizabeth Dillow, Arlington, VA*

60. DAISY, LILY, ROSE
materials patterned paper, coaster (Imagination Project) • gems (Heidi Swapp) • ribbon (American Crafts) • AL Modern Type font • *12 x 12 spread by Mary MacAskill, Calgary, AB*

61. FIVE SIMPLE WAYS (TO LOVE THE EARTH)
materials accordion book (American Traditional Designs) • patterned paper (Tinkering Ink) • vellum • rub-ons, circle tag (Making Memories) • ribbon • corner rounder, circle cutter, circle punch (Creative Memories) • Andale Mono font • *6 x 4¼ mini-album by Margaret Scarbrough, Butte Valley, CA*

62. BE SMART
aba.com/consumer+connection/teachchildren tosave.htm
materials patterned paper (K Memories) • chipboard dollar sign (Basic Grey) • clear text sticker (Joann) • *12 x 12 page by Anna Aspnes, Elmendorf AFB, AK*

63. THE TRUE MEANING OF LIFE
materials patterned paper (MOD for Autumn Leaves) • staples • Thomas Paine font • *12 x 12 page by Elizabeth Dillow, Arlington, VA*

66. TRICYCLE
bike.eague.org
materials album (Danny O for K & Company) • date stickers (EK Success) • transparency (Staples) • paint (Delta) • rub-on (FoofaLa for Autumn Leaves) • AL Modern Type, Rabiohead fonts • *6 x 6 mini-album by Elizabeth Dillow, Arlington, VA*

68. THE MOVE (2006)
materials album (American Crafts) • patterned paper (American Crafts) • maps (Rand McNally) • rubber stamp (Fontwerks) • acrylic stamp (Adornit Carolee's Creations) • rub-ons (Making Memories) • ink (Clearsnap) • Gill Sans Light font • *6 x 6 mini-album by Elizabeth Dillow, Arlington, VA*

70. I USED TO SKATE
materials patterned paper (My Mind's Eye, Sassafras Lass, K & Company) • ghost letters (Heidi Swapp) • alpha letter cards (7Gypsies) • Geo Sans Light font • *5 x 2½ mini-album by Laura Kurz, Baltimore, MD*

71. CAUGHT
materials patterned paper (Scenic Route) • felt stickers (American Crafts) • ribbon (Making Memories) • rubber stamp (Rackel Industries) • *11 x 8½ page by Elizabeth Dillow, Arlington, VA*

72. TEACHING MEMORIES
materials unfinished wooden chalkboard box (Michael's) • patterned paper (FoofaLa for Autumn Leaves) • rub-ons (Making Memories, FoofaLa for Autumn Leaves) • ribbon (Offray) • chalk • pencils • book ring (Staples) • AL Modern Type and Gill Sans Light fonts • *box project by Elizabeth Dillow, Arlington, VA*

74. MOTHER GOOSE, GRANDMA WATSON, AND ME
materials chipboard lacing cards (Cosmo Cricket) • patterned paper, rub-ons, epoxy sticker, tags (FoofaLa for Autumn Leaves) • rub-ons (American Crafts) • ribbon • Bernhard Roman font • *4¼ x 7 accordion album by Elizabeth Dillow, Arlington, VA*

75. TIME FLIES, SO I SCRAPBOOK
materials patterned paper (MOD for Autumn Leaves, Scenic Route) • bird transparency (My Mind's Eye) • American Typewriter font • *12 x 12 page by Elizabeth Dillow, Arlington, VA*

76. REMEMBER
materials album (All My Memories) • patterned paper (Basic Grey) • quote tags (K & Company) • ribbon (MMI) • alpha set circle and square (Making Memories) • mini brads (Queen and Co) • ink (Close To My Heart) • assortment of old buttons, book pages, stamps, game pieces • *4 x 4 mini-album by Anna Aspnes, Elmendorf AFB, AK*

78. 14
materials patterned paper (7Gypsies, KI Memories) • book cloth (Books By Hand) • chipboard book plate (Maya Road) • rubber stamp (Hero Arts) • rub-ons (Making Memories) • ribbon • foam adhesive (All Night Media) • *12 x 12 page by Elizabeth Dillow, Arlington, VA*

79. ALGERIA TO ZIMBABWE
materials patterned paper (Cross-My-Heart) • letter stickers (SEI) • foam adhesive (Scrapbook Adhesives) • corner rounder (Creative Memories) • Futura font • *8½ x 11 page by Margaret Scarbrough, Butte Valley, CA*

June

82. HIKE
americanhiking.org
materials chipboard covers (Junkitz) • vellum (The Paper Company) • rub-ons, stickers, brads (American Crafts) • eyelets (H.A. Kidd & Company Limited) • circle cutter (Creative Memories) • compass • You Can Make Your Own Font font • *6 x 6 mini-album by Mary MacAskill, Calgary, AB*

84. LISA SCOTT-SMITH
materials patterned paper (Danny O for K & Company) • elastic cord (Hancock Fabrics) • eyelets (Making Memories) • postage stamps • *8½ x 11 page by Elizabeth Dillow, Arlington, VA*

85. LET NOTHING STAND IN YOUR WAY
materials patterned paper (American Crafts) • brads (SEI, Karen Foster) • rub-ons (Making Memories, Scrapworks) • paint (Ranger Ink) • ink (Clearsnap) • *12 x 12 page by Mi'Chelle Larsen, Bountiful, UT*

86. COOPERSTOWN
materials chipboard letters (Heidi Swapp) • date sticker (EK Success) • photo border (Snapshot Elements by Rhonna Farrer (www.twopeasinabucket.com) • Geo Sans Light font • *8½ x 11 page by Laura Kurz, Baltimore, MD*

87. ROLLER COASTER
materials patterned paper, epoxy sticker (KI Memories) • Century Gothic font • *12 x 12 page by Elizabeth Dillow, Arlington, VA*

88. SPLIT SECOND
nanpa.org
materials transparency (Staples) • Caecilia Roman, P22 Cezanne fonts • *11 x 8½ page by Elizabeth Dillow, Arlington, VA*

89. SOUTH FORK CRAZY WOMAN
materials map paper (Rand McNally) • chipboard letters, rub-ons, accents (Making Memories) • staples • Abadi MT Condensed Bold, Baskerville fonts • *12 x 12 page by Elizabeth Dillow, Arlington, VA*

July

92. LET'S GO.
materials patterned paper (SandyLion) • chipboard postage shape (Daisy D's) • corner rounder (EK Success) • Gill Sans Light font • *12 x 12 spread by Elizabeth Dillow, Arlington, VA*

93. ART STAMPS
materials rub-ons (Heidi Swapp) • stickers (American Crafts) • Print Clearly font • *8½ x 11 page by Laura Kurz, Baltimore, MD*

94. BY ZIP
materials flip album (Making Memories) • patterned paper (Karen Foster) • rub-ons (Basic Grey) • rubber stamp (Rubber Baby Buggy Bumpers, PSX) • heart brad (Fiskars) • letter stickers (American Crafts) • postage stamp punch (McGill) • Hoefler Text font • *5 x 7 mini-album by Elizabeth Dillow, Arlington, VA*

96. OH, CANADA!
materials stickers, metal tag (Making Memories) • brads, eyelets (American Crafts) • rub-ons (American Crafts, Creative Imaginations) • ribbon (Offray) • AL Messenger font • *4 x 6 mini-album by Mary MacAskill, Calgary, AB*

98. TENDERHEARTED MAMA
materials patterned paper (Basic Grey) • ribbon (Making Memories) • rub-ons (Cross-My-Heart, Making Memories) • Helvetica Neue Light font • *12 x 12 page by Elizabeth Dillow, Arlington, VA*

99. HOWDY LITTLE NEWLYCOME
materials buttons (FoofaLa for Autumn Leaves, Circo) • embroidery thread (DMC) • letter sticker (American Crafts) • Savoye LET font • *12 x 12 page by Elizabeth Dillow, Arlington, VA*

100. DISNEY
materials patterned paper (Cherry Arte) • circle embellishments (KI Memories) • alphabet stickers (K & Company) • buttons • Klill LightTallX, Rosewood Std fonts • *12 x 12 spread by Anna Aspnes, Elmendorf AFB, AK*

101. GOOD PARENTS
materials patterned paper (American Crafts) • transparency (Hambly Screen Prints) • rub-on (Basic Grey) • Thomas Paine font • *12 x 12 page by Elizabeth Dillow, Arlington, VA*

102. OWEN
materials album (Maya Road) • patterned paper (Scenic Route, Anna Griffin, My Mind's Eye, Autumn Leaves) • stickers (American Crafts) • rub-ons, ribbon (Making Memories) • paint (Ranger Inks) • ink (Clearsnap) • *5¾ x 2¾ mini-album by Mi'Chelle Larsen, Bountiful, UT*

August

106. KINDERGARTEN
materials patterned paper (Scenic Route) • letter stickers (Basic Grey) • rub-ons (Autumn Leaves) • pop dots (All Night Media) • Courier font • *11 x 8½ page by Margaret Scarbrough, Butte Valley, CA*

107. INVENTION OF THE CENTURY
materials patterned paper (American Crafts) • rub-ons (7Gypsies, American Crafts) • Helvetica Neue Black, Helvetica Neue Light fonts • *8½ x 11 page by Elizabeth Dillow, Arlington, VA*

108. BRIDGET SOPHIA
materials patterned paper, butterfly brad (MOD for Autumn Leaves) • jewels (K & Company) • rubber stamp (7Gypsies) • Garamond Narrow font • *12 x 12 page by Elizabeth Dillow, Arlington, VA*

109. COLORADO
materials patterned paper (Paper Love Designs) • sticker (7 Gypsies) • font (Century Gothic) • *12 x 12 spread by Elizabeth Dillow*

110. Y IS FOR YUMMY
materials index tab album (Junkitz) • vellum (The Paper Company) • rub-ons, photo corners (American Crafts) • silverware charms, stickers (7Gypsies) • metal tag (Making Memories) • jewelry tag (Avery) • ink (Tsukineko) • Garamond font • *8 x 5½ mini-album by Mary MacAskill, Calgary, AB*

112. COLLECTION
materials rub-ons (American Crafts) • Fontin Sans Small Caps, Gill Sans Light fonts • *12 x 12 page by Elizabeth Dillow, Arlington, VA*

113. NO PLACE LIKE HOME
materials rub-ons, felt flowers (American Crafts) • jewels (K & Company) • chipboard letter (Creative Imaginations) • *12 x 12 page by Elizabeth Dillow, Arlington, VA*

114. TO LOVE A PUG
nationaldogday.com
materials accordion book (Junkitz) • patterned paper and cardstock (Scenic Route) • vellum (The Paper Company) • rub-ons, brads (American Crafts) • page pebble stickers (Making Memories) • threads (MAMBI) • punch (Marvy Uchida) • Journaling Hand font • *5 x 6 mini-album by Mary MacAskill, Calgary, AB*

115. 1966 FAMILY REUNION
materials acrylic frame (Making Memories) • chipboard letter (Heidi Swapp) • fabric label (MAMBI) • rub-ons (Autumn Leaves) • Times New Roman font • *8 x 8 spread by Laura Kurz, Baltimore, MD*

September

118. I WISH I KNEW
materials rub-ons, metal book plate (Basic Grey) • digital frame (Snap Shot by Rhonna Farrer www.twopeasinabucket.com)) • AL Modern Type font • *8½ x 11 page by Elizabeth Dillow, Arlington, VA*

119. GOOGLE
materials patterned paper (KI Memories) • circle stickers (Gartner Studios) • glitter glue (Ranger Ink) • Book Antiqua, Typewriter Rough fonts • *8½ x 11 page by Elizabeth Dillow, Arlington, VA*

120. SEPTEMBER 11
materials album (American Crafts) • patterned paper (Danny O for K & Company) • postage stamp • flag pin • postage stamp punch (McGill) • Cochin font • *6 x 6 mini-album by Elizabeth Dillow, Arlington, VA*

122. A READING TRADITION
materials patterned paper (American Crafts) • rub-ons (Li'l Davis Designs) • ribbon (Making Memories) • foam adhesive (All Night Media) • Arial Narrow font • *8½ x 11 page by Margaret Scarbrough, Butte Valley, CA*

123. A FRIEND LIKE THIS
materials patterned paper (FoofaLa for Autumn Leaves, Making Memories) • rubber stamps (Hero Arts) • ink (Clearsnap) • Baskerville Old Face font • *8½ x 11 page by Elizabeth Dillow, Arlington, VA*

124. BE LONGING?
digital materials Photoshop CS2 (Adobe Systems) • patterned paper (Chloe's Closet Paperie by Anna Aspnes (www.designerdigitals.com) • girl custom shape (Photoshop CS2) • stock photos (www.sxc.hu) • *12 x 12 page by Anna Aspnes, Calgary, AB*

125. THANK YOU
materials film negative transparency (Karen Russell for Creative Imaginations) • chipboard star (Heidi Swapp) • metal charm (Making Memories) • map (Rand McNally) • Gill Sans Light font • *8½ x 11 spread by Elizabeth Dillow, Arlington, VA*

126. HOMER, ALASKA
materials album (JoAnn's) • patterned paper (MME) • patterned paper, frames, accents, ribbon (Wild Asparagus) • paint (MME) • twill tape • fabric labels (Li'l Davis Designs) • brads (Queen & Co.) • rings (Junkitz) • metal alphas (Making Memories) • flower (Doodlebug Designs) • *5 X 7 mini-album by Anna Aspnes, Elmendorf AFB, AK*

127. NEIGHBORS
natgoodneighborday.org
materials patterned paper (Danny O for K & Company) • rub-ons (Making Memories) • paper flowers (Prima Marketing Inc.) • waxed thread (Books By Hand) • dictionary paper (Webster's Dictionary) • 8½ x 11 page by Elizabeth Dillow, Arlington, VA

128. HECTOR THE COLLECTOR
materials patterned paper (Scenic Route, a regular notebook) • keys (Making Memories) • ghost letters (Heidi Swapp) • chipboard letter (Scenic Route) • fabric tabs (Scrapworks) • rub-ons (Scrapworks, American Crafts, Making Memories) • ink (Clearsnap) • 8½ x 11 spread by Mi'Chelle Larsen, Bountiful, UT

129. THE PIANO LESSON
materials patterned paper (Chatterbox) • rub-ons (Autumn Leaves) • metal charm (Making Memories) • ribbon • 8½ x 11 page by Elizabeth Dillow, Arlington, VA

October

132. WALK
materials album (American Crafts) • patterned paper (MOD for Autumn Leaves, KI Memories) • acrylic stamp (Autumn Leaves) • rub-ons (Art Warehouse by Creative Imaginations, Autumn Leaves) • ribbon • Stone Sans ITC-TT Sem., Gill Sans Light fonts • photos by Kattie Spies and Helen Dickerson • 6 x 6 mini-album by Elizabeth Dillow, Arlington, VA

134. GRANDMA WATSON'S BUTTONS
materials frame (Target) • patterned paper (source unknown) • rub-ons (FoofaLa for Autumn Leaves) • Goudy Old Style font • 10 x 10 frame by Elizabeth Dillow, Arlington, VA

135. SHARE YOUR HAPPINESS
worldcardmakingday.com
materials patterned paper (Doodlebug Designs, Making Memories, My Mind's Eye, Heidi Grace Designs, Provo Craft, Die Cuts With a View, Paper Fever, The Paper Patch, NRN Designs, SEI, KI Memories) • vellum (The Paper Company) • brads (American Crafts, Making Memories) • chipboard numbers (Scenic Route) • stickers (EK Success, Provo Craft, Making Memories) • tape (Heidi Swapp) • die cuts (Cricut by Provo Craft) • paint (Pebbles, Inc., Making Memories) • rub-ons, flower (American Crafts) • 8 x 5 mini-album by Mary MacAskill, Calgary, AB

136. THE BOOKS THAT CHANGED MY LIFE
nationalbook.org
materials bookmark sleeves (Craft Supplies For Less, Inc.) • patterned paper (Scenic Route, MOD for Autumn Leaves, KI Memories, FoofaLa for Autumn Leaves) • rub-ons (7Gypsies, Basic Grey, Hambly Screen Prints) • photo turns (Making Memories) • jewels (K & Company) • bird transparency (My Mind's Eye) • chipboard brackets (Making Memories) • ribbon (Basic Grey) • paper clips • metal charms (The Creative Block) • rubber stamp (7Gypsies) • die cut flower (Paper House Productions) • label (7Gypsies) • postage stamps • book ring (Staples) • Helvetica Neue Ultra Light, Bell MT fonts • 2½ x 7 bookmarks by Elizabeth Dillow, Arlington, VA

138. HOONIE
materials patterned paper (Colorbök, Adornit Carolee's Creations, FoofaLa for Autumn Leaves, PSX Paper Designs, Rusty Pickle, 7Gypsies, Anna Griffin, Cross-My-Heart, Making Memories) • chipboard letter (Making Memories) • alphabet tabs (Autumn Leaves) • eyelet (Creative Imaginations) • corner rounder (Creative Memories) • book ring (Staples) • chipboard • ribbon • Gadget, Times fonts • 3 x 8½ hanging mini-album by Margaret Scarbrough, Butte Valley, CA

139. TIME
timeday.org
materials patterned paper (KI Memories) • rub-ons (Imaginisce, American Crafts) • chipboard circle (Bazzill Basics Paper) clear tabs (Avery) • ink (Clearsnap) • 12 x 12 page by Elizabeth Dillow, Arlington, VA

140. CHARACTER COUNTS
materials journaling curtain (Stemma) • Copperplate Gothic font • 8½ x 11 page by Elizabeth Dillow, Arlington, VA

141. GAMER
millionminute.com
materials patterned paper (Peggy Tales) • letter stickers (Scrapworks) • foam adhesive (All Night Media) • arrow punch (Fiskars) • corner rounder (Creative Memories) • Century Gothic font • 11 x 8½ page by Margaret Scarbrough, Butte Valley, CA

November

144. BONFIRE NIGHT
materials patterned paper (Rusty Pickle, Sweetwater) • transparency (Creative Imaginations) • quote strip (K & Company) • ink (Close To My Heart) • brush sets/digital stamps (Boho Flourish Frame Brush Set by Michelle Coleman (www.scraparist.com), distressed frame by Rhonna Farrer and Autumn Leaves Designing with Digital Book and CD) • stock photos (www.sxc.hu) • 12 x 12 spread by Anna Aspnes, Elmendorf AFB, AK

145. SESAME STREET
materials patterned paper (Sassafras Lass) • rub-ons (KI Memories, Autumn Leaves) • rubber stamp (Heidi Swapp) • ink (Close To My Heart) • corner rounder • Splendid 66 font • 8½ x 11 page by Laura Kurz, Baltimore, MD

146. A SWOOP AND A DART
ilovetowriteday.org
materials binder (Russell•Hazel) • patterned paper, tags (Basic Grey) • rubber stamp (Paper Inspirations Ma Vinci's Reliquary) • paint (Delta) • ink (Memories) • rub-ons (Making Memories, Autumn Leaves) • Typewriter Rough, Garamond Narrow fonts • 8½ x 11 album by Elizabeth Dillow, Arlington, VA

148. LIFE
digital materials photo book (Shutterfly) • brush sets (Hipster Plumes MegaPak by Anna Aspnes (www.designerdigitals.com)) • Courier New, Arial fonts • 12 x 12 photo book by Anna Aspnes, Elmendorf AFB, AK

150. THIS MOMENT
materials patterned paper (SEI, Basic Grey, Sassafrass Lass) • eyelets (Making Memories) • rub-ons (American Crafts) • 8½ x 11 page by Mi'Chelle Larsen, Bountiful, UT

151. OSU GIRL
materials metal letters (Making Memories) • alphabet stickers (American Crafts) • 8½ x 11 page by Elizabeth Dillow, Arlington, VA

152. FAMILY RESEMBLANCE
materials rub-ons (American Crafts, Autumn Leaves) • rubber stamp (Fontwerks) • ink (Clearsnap, Tsukineko) • Times New Roman font • 8½ x 11 page by Laura Kurz, Baltimore, MD

153. HELLO MY NAME IS (PAGE)
worldhelloday.org
materials patterned paper (Luxe Designs) • metal tab (Making Memories) • Helvetica Neue Light, Riverside, 2Peas DW Oh Baby fonts • 12 x 12 page by Elizabeth Dillow, Arlington, VA

153. HELLO MY NAME IS (CARD)
materials patterned paper (Luxe Designs) • envelope (Gartner Studios) • Helvetica Neue Light, Riverside, 2Peas DW Oh Baby fonts • 4 x 6 card by Elizabeth Dillow, Arlington, VA

December

156. I {HEART} COOKIES
materials patterned paper (Treehouse Designs, SEI, Anna Griffin, Basic Grey, MOD for Autumn Leaves) • ribbon (May Arts) • corner rounder (EK Success) • Crop-A-Dile (We R Memory Keepers) • Little Days, Times New Roman fonts • handmade album by Mi'Chelle Larsen, Bountiful, UT

158. G
materials album (Bazzill Basics Paper) • patterned paper, rubber stamp (7Gypsies) • rub-on (MAMBI) • circle punch (Marvy Uchida) • heart punch (EK Success) • 2Peas Vegetable Soup, Rabiohead fonts • 6 x 12 album by Elizabeth Dillow, Arlington, VA

160. THE COMFORTS OF HOME
materials album (Creative Imaginations) • patterned paper (Flip Flops, Scenic Route) • tag, rub-ons (Making Memories) • digital brushes (Old Stamps by Rhonna Farrer www.twopeasinabucket.com)) • ink (Clearsnap) • Times New Roman font • 5 x 7 accordion album by Mi'Chelle Larsen, Bountiful, UT

162. PUZZLE
materials patterned paper (American Crafts) • ribbon, letter (Making Memories) • corner rounder (EK Success) • heart punch (EK Success) • 12 x 12 page by Elizabeth Dillow, Arlington, VA

163. THE BOXING DAY FIASCO
materials patterned paper (SEI) • screw snap (Making Memories) • letter stickers (American Crafts) • corner rounder (Marvy Uchida) • Sansumi, Billo fonts • 12 x 12 page by Mary MacAskill, Calgary, AB

164. SWEET, SWEET TWIX
materials transparency (Staples) • rub-ons, chipboard letters, brads (American Crafts) • ribbon (Offray) • photo corners (Canson) • Suede font • 12 x 12 page by Mary MacAskill, Calgary, AB

165. THIS YEAR
materials patterned paper (Basic Grey) • number stickers (Making Memories) • acrylic stamp (Technique Tuesday) • paint (Delta) • ribbon (Making Memories, Offray) • photo by Deb Karahalis • 8½ x 11 page by Elizabeth Dillow, Arlington, VA

Elizabeth Dillow is a contributing editor for *Simple Scrapbooks* magazine (and a 2006 *Creating Keepsakes* Hall of Fame winner) who doesn't remember a time when she wasn't taking photos of her family. She loves history, storytelling, music, art, and baseball, and enjoys hanging out at bookstores. She thought up this book while living in Colorado Springs, Colorado, completed all the pages and projects in Mountain House, California, and now lives in Arlington, Virginia, with her husband Matt and three little pixie girls: Madeline, Grace, and Bridget.